D0806853

101
PAPER PLANES

hinkler

Published by Hinkler Books Pty Ltd
45–55 Fairchild Street
Heatherton Victoria 3202 Australia
www.hinkler.com.au

© Hinkler Books Pty Ltd 2013

Author: Dean Mackey
Illustrations: Brijbasi Art Press
Cover Design: Sam Grimmer
Typesetting: MPS Limited
Prepress: Graphic Print Group

ISBN: 978 1 7435 2083 3

Printed and bound in China

Contents

Introduction

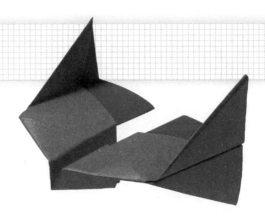

Paper planes

First of all, thank you for buying this book. I hope you have fun making these designs on the cool paper!

Paper planes are a one-way ticket back to your childhood. Paper planes are the perfect hobby or interest for people of all ages, backgrounds and levels of expertise. Plane making is both stimulating and relaxing. It costs virtually nothing, needs no equipment and is a low-tech way to have a lot of fun. You can choose to make designs as easy or as relatively difficult as you wish; either way making paper planes gives you a real sense of achievement. Create them on your own, as a family or as a small group and see how fast, high and long they can fly. Above all, have fun with them!

A brief history of paper planes

The first real plane was designed, built and flown in 1903 by the Wright brothers. As far as I can tell, the earliest documented paper plane followed ten years later, in 1913. I am still searching for earlier paper plane designs; I have read about some from as early as 700 AD!

Some of the first pilots, the 'Early Birds', created some very nice paper plane designs. A standout is Percy Pierce. His patented designs appeared in issues of American women's fashion magazines McCall's and The Delineator in the 1920s. The planes were quite striking, and fairly complex to assemble.

During the 1940s, great advances occurred in aviation. Planes flew faster and higher, and were more reliable than ever. In this decade the jet engine was born, and all metal planes reigned supreme. As a consequence, the increased knowledge of avionics also improved paper planes. Paper planes became so popular that designs were even featured on cereal boxes. A key designer of the day was Wallis Rigby, who is credited with creating the 'tab and slot' method. His planes appeared in newspapers, thrilling readers with their realistic detail. Even today they are a lot of fun to make and fly.

The *Great International Paper Airplane Book,* published in 1967, introduced the concept of laminate paper planes, which were made popular by Dr Yasuaki Ninomiya of Japan in his famous and fantastic Whitewings series. Capable of greater speeds, heights and variety of shapes, some of the models were even propelled by a rubber band launcher, which could catapult them high enough to ride thermals!

A further significant development occurred in the 1970s when Americans Richard Kline and Floyd Fogleman came up with a new airfoil design using paper planes as a test bed. Their unique wing shape could also change its thickness, and they eventually patented the concept, which was quite a feat! Their 1985 book, *The Ultimate Paper Airplane*, provides plans for seven different models of this ground-breaking design.

Paper plane competitions

The first international paper plane competition was held in 1967, sponsored and conducted by Scientific American. The competition brought together various styles and forms of paper plane making from all over the world, which were subsequently published in the *Great International Paper Airplane Book*. The book became a bestseller and many of its designs are among those that are most known today.

In 1985 the second international paper plane contest was held. Conducted by the editors of Science 86 magazine, it demonstrated how many advances had been made since the first contest eighteen years previously.

The World Record

Takuo Toda, Chairman of the Japan Origami Airplane Association, is the current title holder of the Guinness World Record for time aloft of a paper plane. He set the record in April 2009, with a time of 27.9 seconds. Prior to Mr Toda breaking the World Record, Ken Blackburn, an aeronautical engineer living in Laurel Hill, Florida, held the record of 27.6 seconds for over 10 years!

A note on paper

These planes were initially designed for my first book, *Fold & Fly Paper Planes*, which has 50 planes for use with A4 or US Standard-sized paper. *101 Paper Planes* features six key designs from that book, only it uses paper that is two-thirds the size of A4.

Sometimes paper planes don't fly as well when you reduce or increase the size. It can be due to the weight of the paper you use or the change of the balance of the plane. The only way I can tell if it will fly is to make the plane and fly it, so that is what I did! Here are the results: six excellent designs that you can make with the paper included in the book.

I can understand why five of them fly well, even at this size. But the Alien Lander still confuses me as to why it can fly at all! It is a strange plane: a delta biplane. I have never seen a real one, but who knows? Maybe you will get inspired by this design and make one to fly in.

We have included six blank planes templates that you can use as practice planes or you can decorate and design however you want! Incidentally, if you learn these folds, you can use A4 or US Standard paper to make the planes and never run out of flying fun!

About the author

Growing up in Iowa, Dean Mackey always enjoyed flying paper planes. Some of his earliest memories are of flying paper planes off the porch and watching them soar over the cliff across the street. His older siblings taught him a few designs, and he learnt a few more from the venerable *Great International Paper Airplane Book*.

Dean's skills lay dormant until the year 2000, when he volunteered to work at 'Space Day' in Tewksbury, Massachusetts. Researching new designs, Dean was amazed at what he found on the internet. As well as experimenting with his own designs, he started collecting web links that talented people had put online for all to enjoy. A few years later, he launched The Online Paper Airplane Museum, featuring over 800 free paper plane designs, personal reviews of paper plane books, and many other items related to paper planes.

Visit The Online Paper Airplane Museum at http://www.theonlinepaperairplanemuseum.com. Questions or comments can be sent to Dean at deanmackey@gmail.com.

This book is dedicated to Katie (Schmoopie) Mackey.

Aviation Glossary

AILERON
A movable panel at the rear edge of each aeroplane wing; the aileron can be raised or lowered and cause the plane to bank left or right.

AIRFOIL
The shape of the wing as seen from the side; it is the shape of the wing that causes a plane to lift.

CANARD
A small wing that sits forward of the main wings on the fuselage of a plane.

DIHEDRAL
The position of the wings on a plane relative to the fuselage. If the wings are raised relative to the fuselage, the dihedral is positive. If the wings are lowered, the dihedral is negative.

No dihedral   Positive dihedral   Negative dihedral

ELEVATOR
The control flaps at the rear of an aircraft; the elevator can be raised or lowered and cause the plane to ascend or descend.

FUSELAGE
The main body of a plane; the wings and tail attach to the fuselage of the plane.

RUDDER

A vertical airfoil at the tail of a plane used for steering; the rudder can be moved left or right and cause the plane to move right or left.

SPOILER

A small airfoil, usually found on the rear of a racing car. On the planes in this book, a spoiler is intended to increase lift.

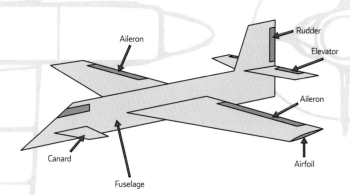

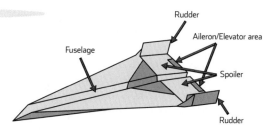

Folding Glossary

FLIP FOLD	Fold up along the result of a previous fold.	
INSIDE REVERSE FOLD	The corner of an existing fold is creased, pushed in and folded on the inside.	
MOUNTAIN FOLD	Fold sides together so paper forms a ∧ shape.	
PRESS	Use your fingers to push the paper in the correct direction.	
PRESS FOLD	Bring two creases together and press down the excess paper that is curved between them to create a new crease.	
REVERSE FOLD	The corner of an existing fold is creased, reversed and folded over to the outside.	

SQUASH FOLD	Start with at least two layers of paper. Make creases in the top layer. Lift the top layer, move it across and then press down on the creases.	
TAP	Use your finger and tap where indicated to set off a preset series of folds.	
TRIM	The final adjustments to a paper plane so that it flies straight and true. This may involve adjustments to the ailerons, elevator and rudder.	
VALLEY FOLD	Fold sides together so paper forms a V shape.	

Standard

Here is a plane design that is truly international. I recently met a Russian woman who had made this in her childhood. It is exactly the same design I learned growing up in Iowa. Capable of fast speed and accuracy, the Standard will streak across the sky!

1

Begin with a sheet of paper using the Standard template.

2

Fold the left side over to and even with the right side.

3

Fold the top right corner down to the left side.

4

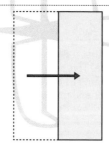

Fold the right side over to the left side as shown.

5

Fold again from the right side over to the left side as shown.

6

Flip over, from left to right.

Standard

7

Fold the top left corner down to the right side.

8

Fold from the left side over to the right side as shown.

9

Fold the left side over to the right side again, as shown.

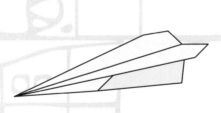

Unfold, and pop up the wings to give a slight dihedral, as shown. It may also need a little up elevator. This plane will fly far and fast if you grasp it along the fuselage and throw it as hard as you can!

Javelin

Much like the track and field spear this plane is named after, the Javelin is truly meant for distance competitions.

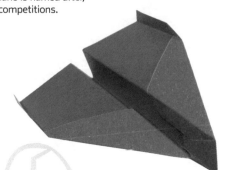

1

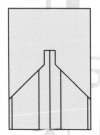

Begin with a sheet of paper using the Javelin template.

2

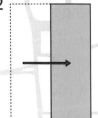

Fold the left side over to and even with the right side.

3

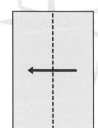

Unfold.

4

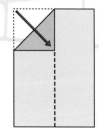

Fold the top left corner down.

5

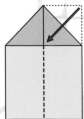

Repeat the same fold with the top right corner.

6

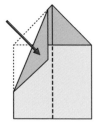

Fold the left side in, stopping 0.9cm (0.4in) from the centre crease.

7

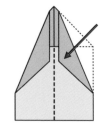

Repeat on the right side, stopping 0.9cm (0.4 inch) from the centre crease.

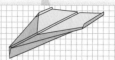

8

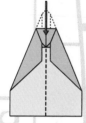

Fold the top down to the line as shown.

9

Fold the left side over to and even with the right side.

10

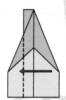

Fold the top wing to the left, starting at the top right corner and keeping the bottom edge even.

11

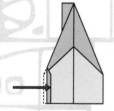

Fold the left side in 0.5cm (0.12in).

12

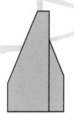

Flip over, from left to right.

13

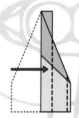

Fold the left side over to the right side, keeping the left edge even with the wing beneath it.

14

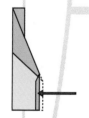

Fold the right side in 0.5cm (0.12in).

This is a great and graceful distance flyer. It may need a little up elevator, but in still air, the Javelin will fly straight and far!

Afterburner

An afterburner is a component of some jet engines, placed after the main engine. Extra fuel is injected into the afterburner and burned for increased thrust. In this paper aeroplane, a spoiler is placed near the end to increase lift. Adding the spoiler to the stabilisers also makes it more stable!

1

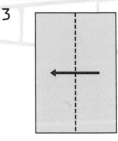

Begin with a sheet of paper using the Afterburner template.

2

Fold the left side over to and even with the right side.

3

Unfold.

4

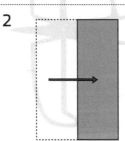

Fold the top edge down to the bottom edge.

5

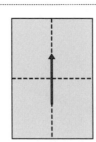

Unfold.

6

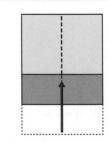

Fold the bottom edge up to the centre crease.

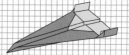

7

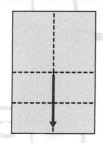

Unfold.

8

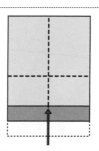

Fold the bottom edge up to the crease just created.

9

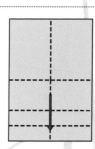

Unfold.

10

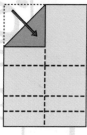

Fold the top left corner down to the vertical centre crease.

11

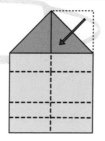

Fold the top right corner down to the vertical centre crease.

12

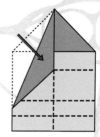

Fold the top left angled side over to the vertical centre crease as shown.

13

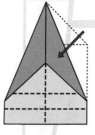

Fold the top right angled side over to the vertical centre crease as shown.

14

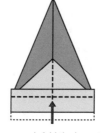

Now squash fold the lowest crease up to the one above it.

15

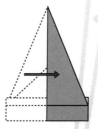

Fold the left side over to and even with the right side.

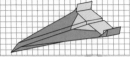

Afterburner

16

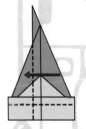

Fold the top wing over to the left, leaving 1.4cm (0.5in) for the fuselage.

17

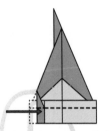

Fold the left side over 1.4cm (0.5in).

18

Flip, from left to right.

19

Fold the left side over so that the left side on top matches the fold below.

20

Fold the right side over 1.4cm (0.5 inch).

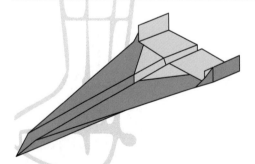

The Afterburner's additional reinforcement in the back provides it with extra lift and accuracy. Use it wisely!

Mighty Mite

This little aeroplane is a great performer! Compact and strong, it can take a lot of punishment and still keep flying. Give it a try and you will see how the Mighty Mite earned its name!

1

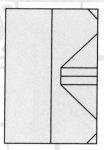

Begin with a sheet of paper using the Mighty Mite template.

2

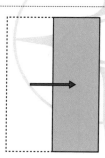

Fold the left side over to and even with the right side.

3

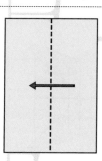

Unfold.

4

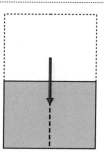

Fold the top edge down to and even with the bottom edge.

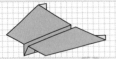

Mighty Mite

5

Unfold.

6

Fold the left side over to the centre vertical crease.

7

Fold the top left corner down to the intersection as shown.

8

Fold the bottom left corner up to the intersection as shown.

9

Flip fold the left side over to the intersection.

10

Flip fold the left side over again.

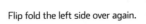

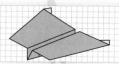

11

Flip over, from left to right.

12

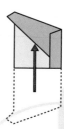

Fold the bottom edge up to and even with the top edge.

13

Fold the top layer down, leaving 1.2cm (0.4in) for the fuselage.

14

Flip over, from left to right.

15

Fold the top edge down to and even with the bottom edge.

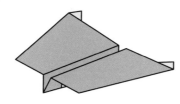

Put a small positive dihedral on the wings, and you have your Mighty Mite!

Scoop

As you can see, the Scoop has a lot in common with the Mighty Mite. Although the Scoop is not as tough, it is still a good flyer to have fun with!

1

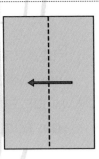

Begin with a sheet of paper using the Scoop template.

2

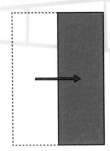

Fold the left side over to and even with the right side.

3

Unfold.

4

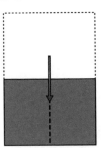

Fold the top edge down to and even with the bottom edge.

Scoop

5

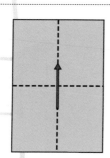

Unfold.

6

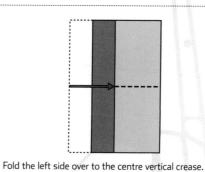

Fold the left side over to the centre vertical crease.

7

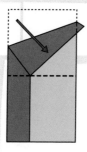

Fold the top left corner down to the intersection.

8

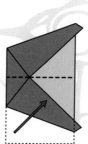

Fold the bottom left corner up to the intersection.

9

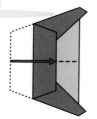

Fold the left side over to the right side, pivoting along the intersection.

10

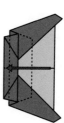

Take the right edge just created and fold it to the left 2cm (0.85in) as shown.

21

Scoop

11

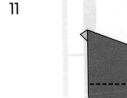

Flip over, from left to right.

12

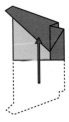

Fold the bottom edge up to and even with the top edge.

13

Fold the top layer down so that the right side of the fold is even with the bottom edge.

14

Flip over, from left to right.

15

Fold the top edge down to and even with the bottom edge.

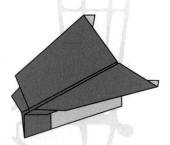

Elevate the Scoop's wings to a slight positive dihedral and it is ready for take-off!

Alien Lander

If spacemen need a scout craft, so do any alien races we may encounter. This plane looks like it came straight out of a science-fiction comic book. But it's even better than that because it really flies!

1

Begin with a sheet of paper using the Alien Lander template.

2

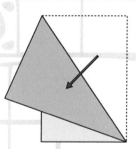

Fold the right side over, creasing from corner to corner.

3

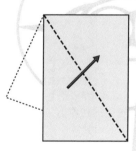

Unfold.

4

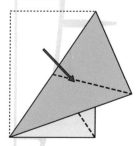

Fold the left side over, creasing from corner to corner.

5

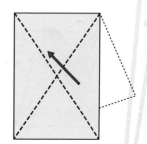

Unfold.

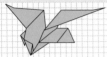

Alien Lander

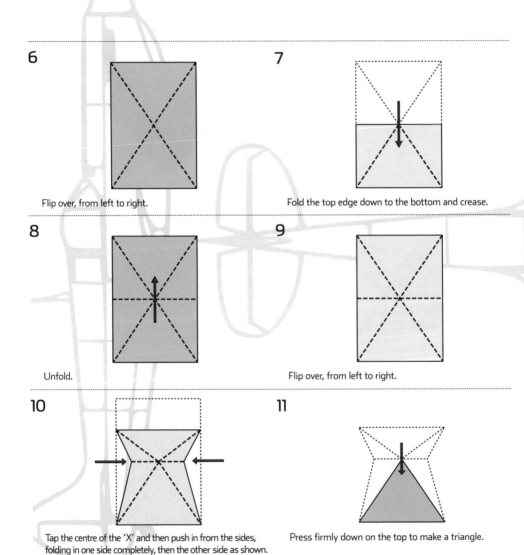

6

Flip over, from left to right.

7

Fold the top edge down to the bottom and crease.

8

Unfold.

9

Flip over, from left to right.

10

Tap the centre of the 'X' and then push in from the sides, folding in one side completely, then the other side as shown.

11

Press firmly down on the top to make a triangle.

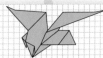

Alien Lander

12

Fold the point down 2.7cm (1.12in) and crease.

13

Fold the point back up.

14

Fold the left side over to and even with the right side and crease.

15

Unfold.

16

Flip over, from left to right.

17

Fold the top layer on the left over to the right 2.2cm (0.85in).

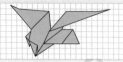

Alien Lander

18

Fold the top left layer over to and even with the centre crease as shown.

19

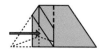

Fold the lower left layer over to and even with the centre crease as shown.

20

Fold the top layer on the right over to the left 2.2cm (0.85in).

21

Fold the top right layer over to and even with the centre crease as shown.

22

Fold the lower right layer over to the centre crease as shown.

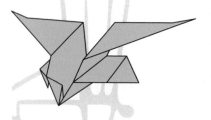

The Alien Lander may need a little twisting up of the ends in order to operate in our atmosphere. It will make a nice three-point landing on our planet!

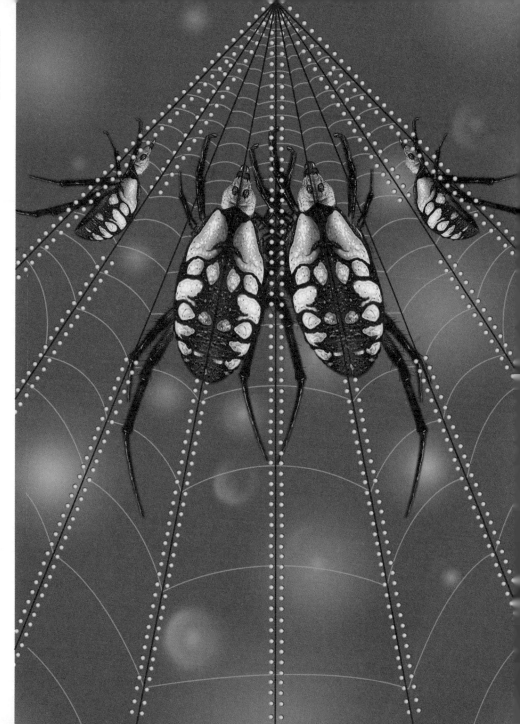

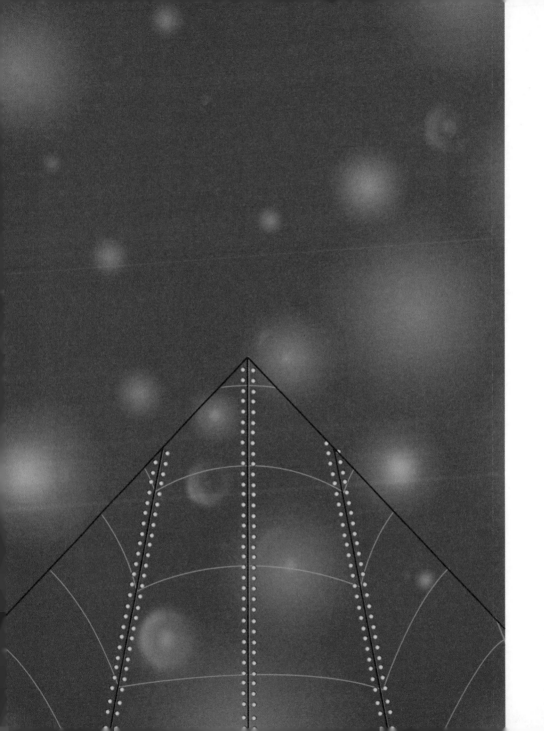

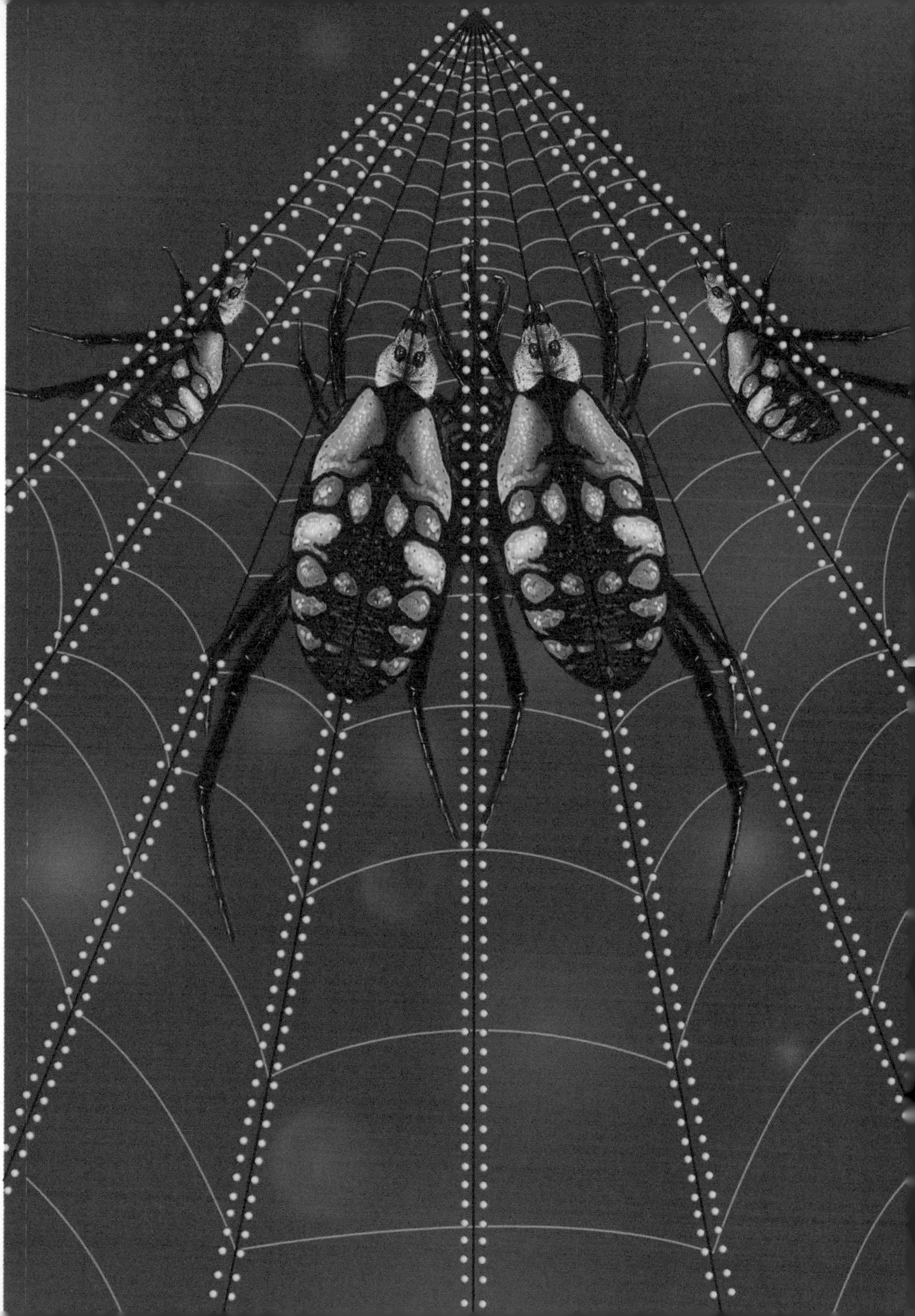

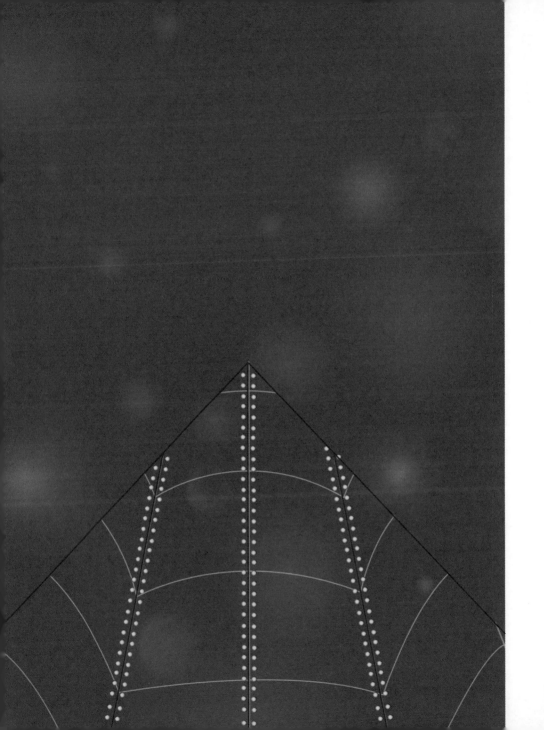

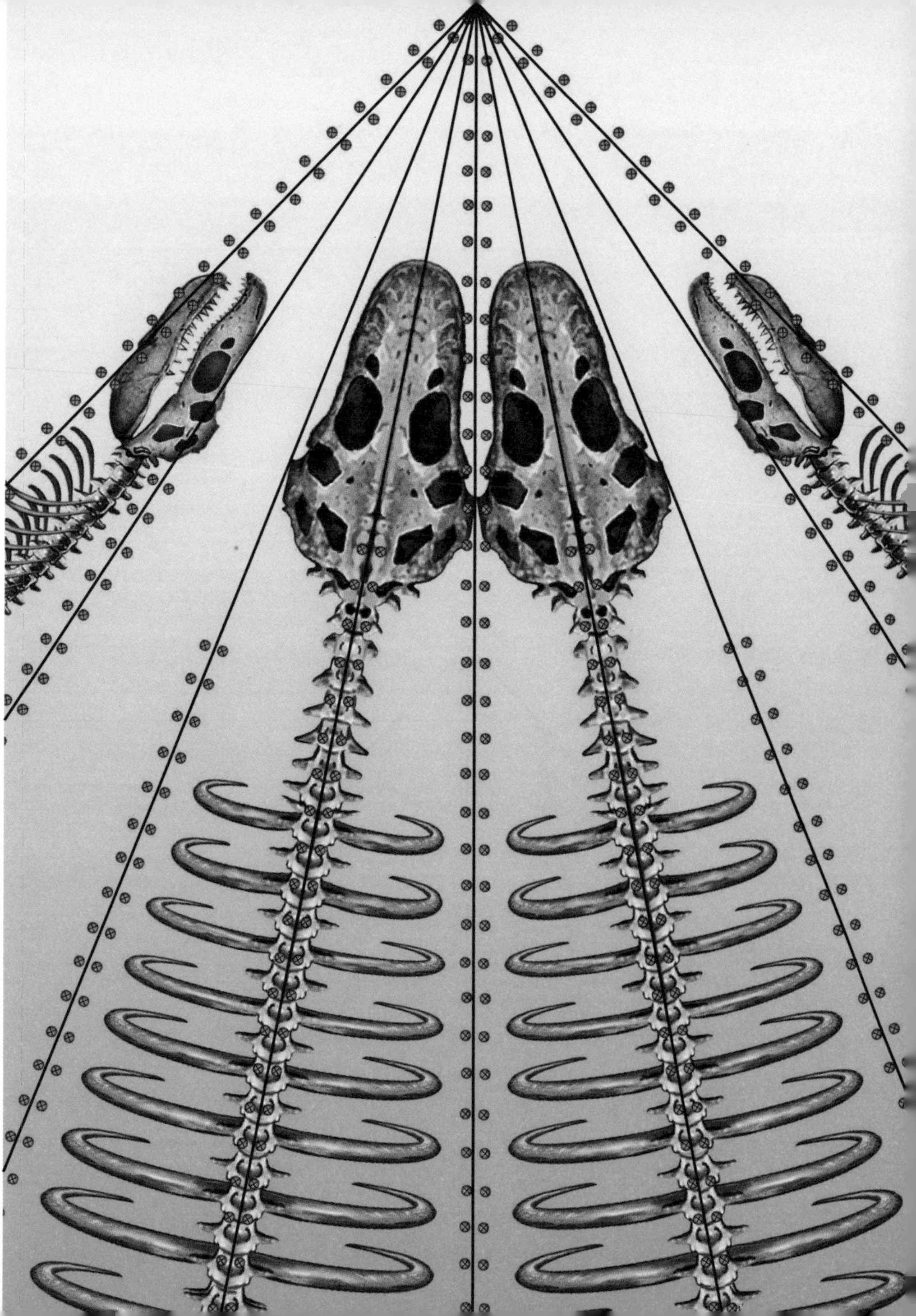

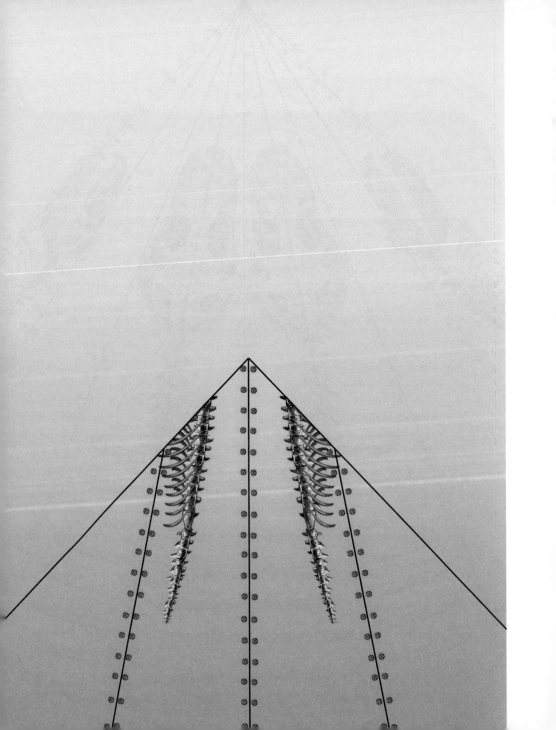

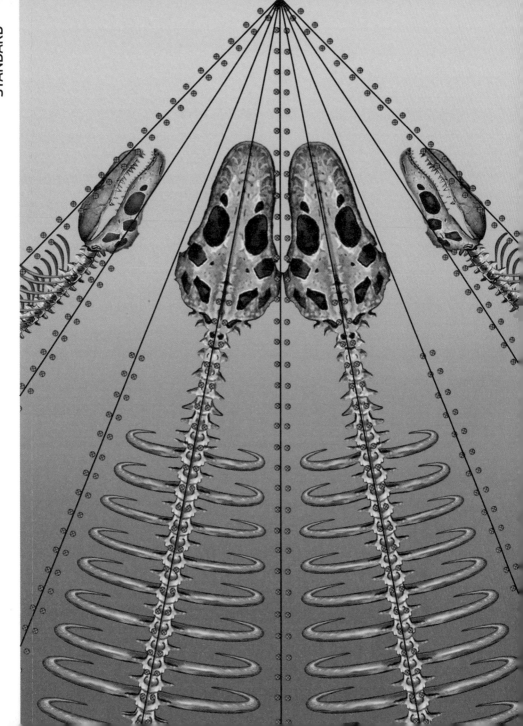

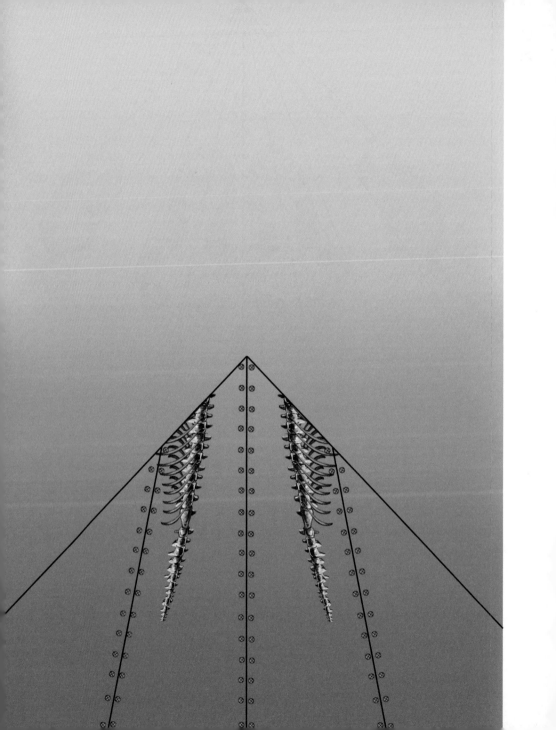

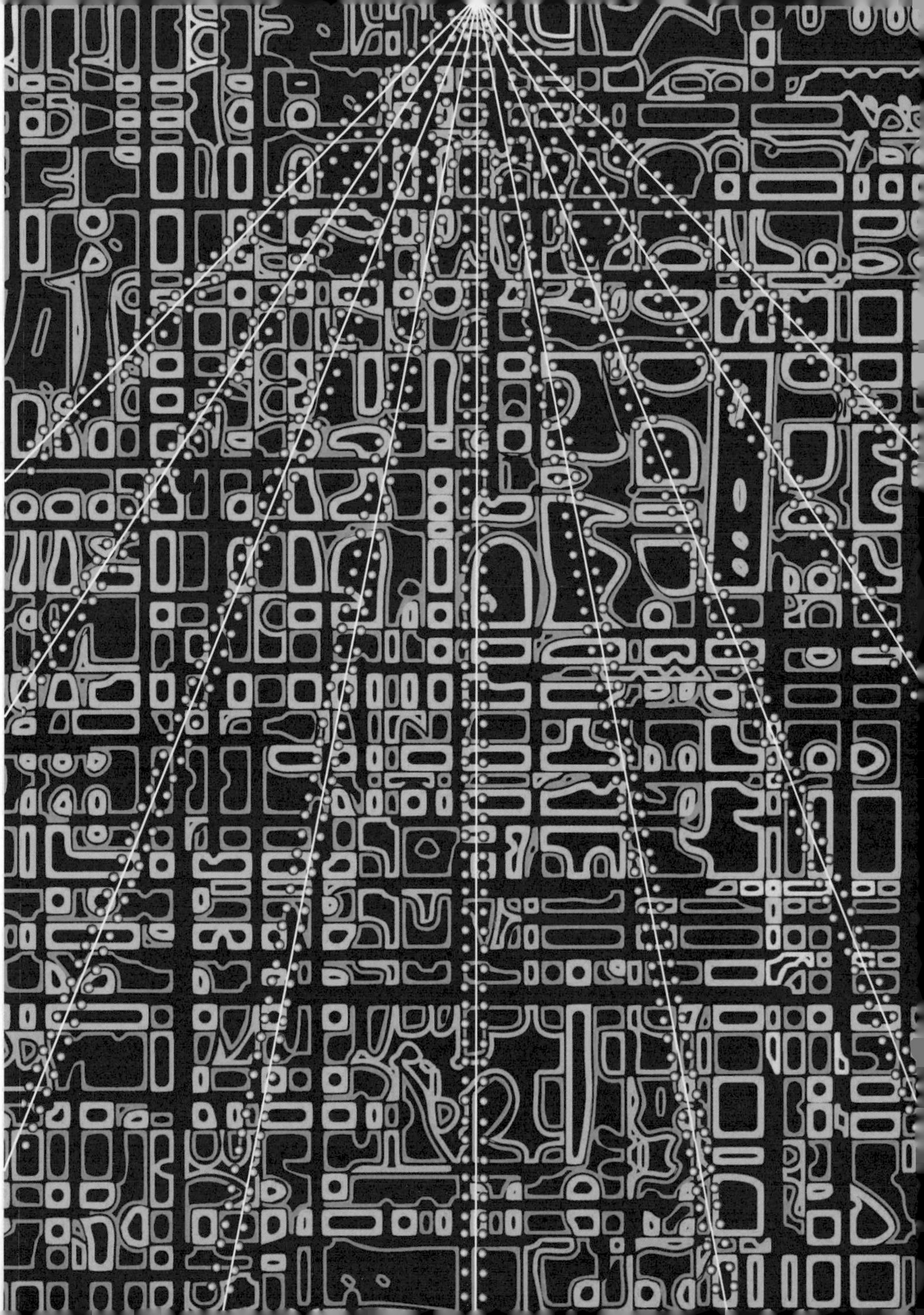

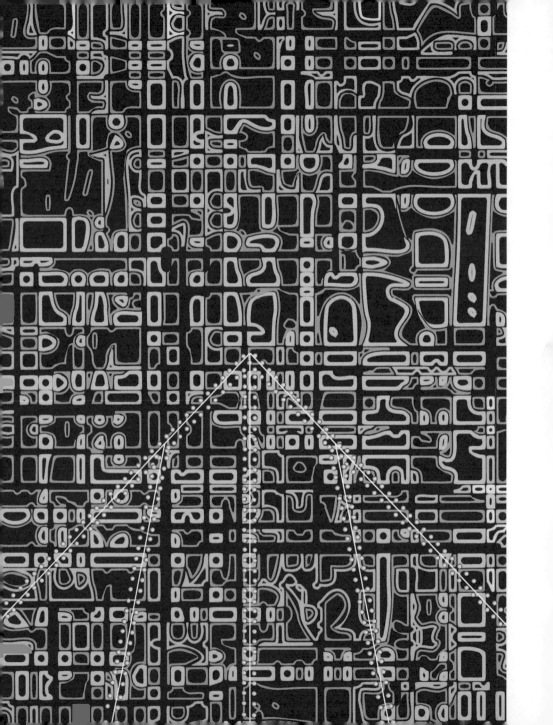

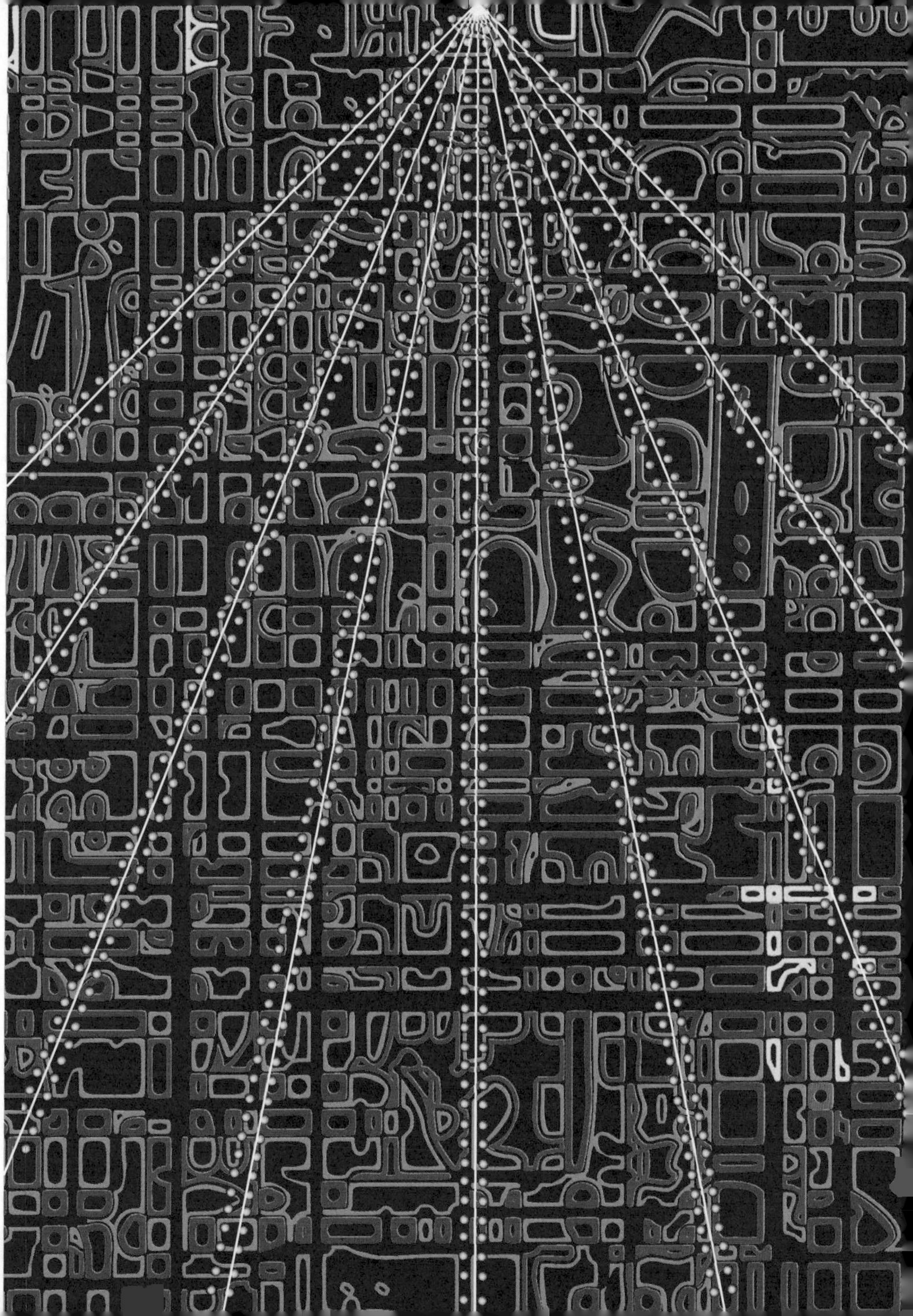

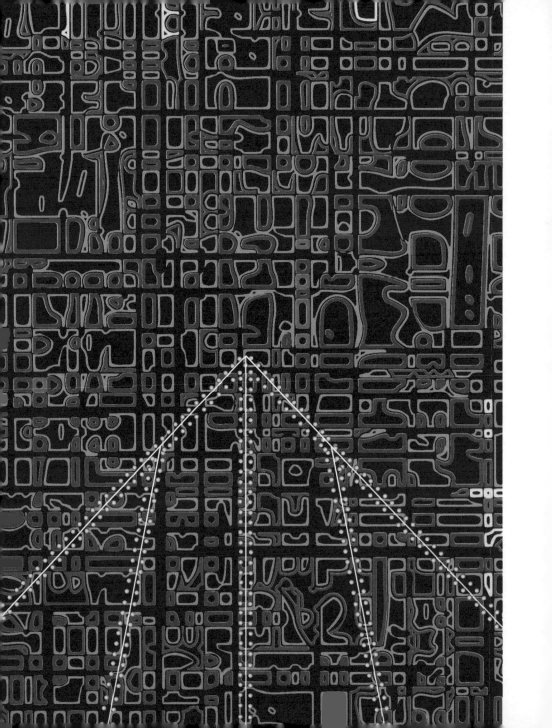

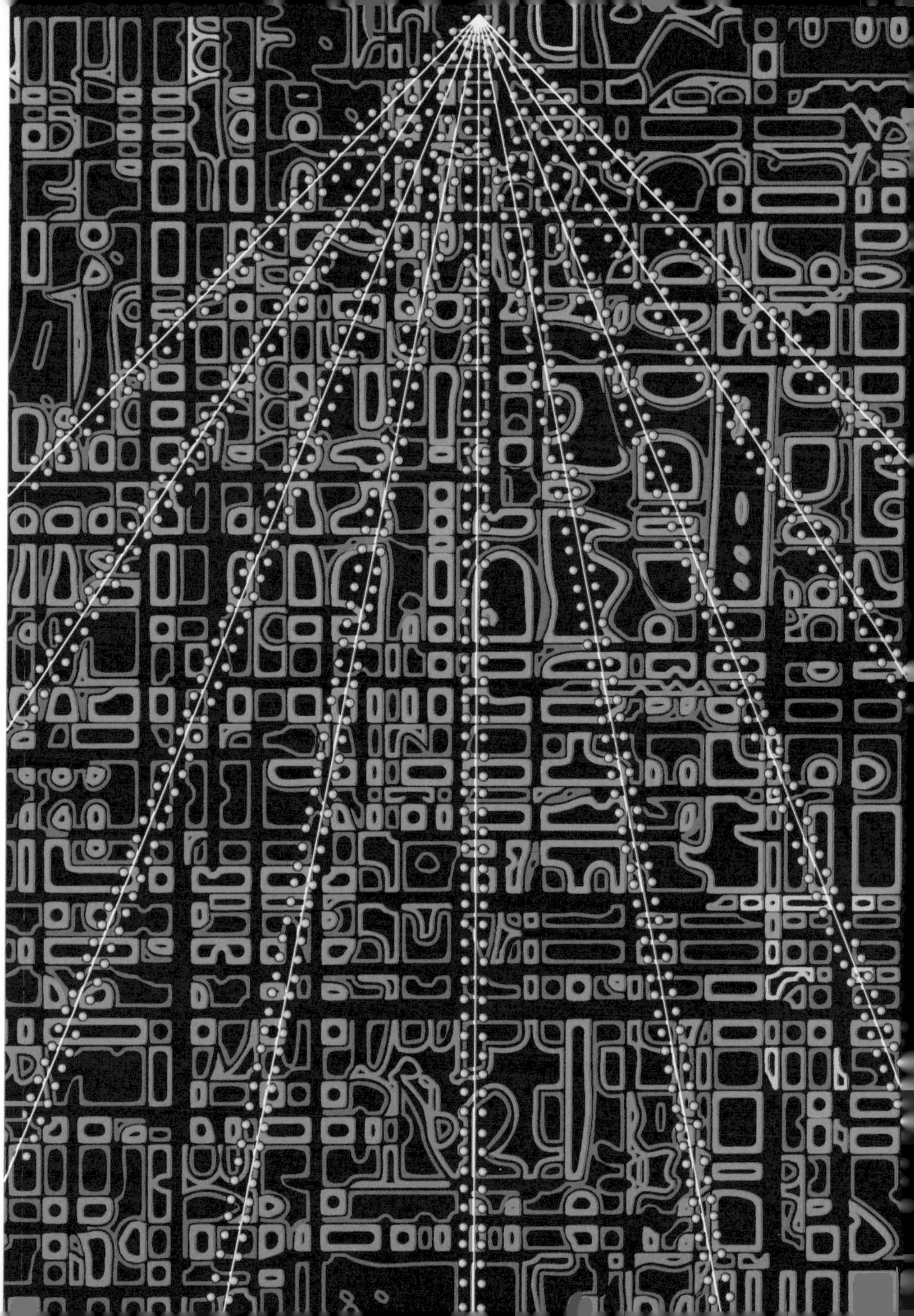

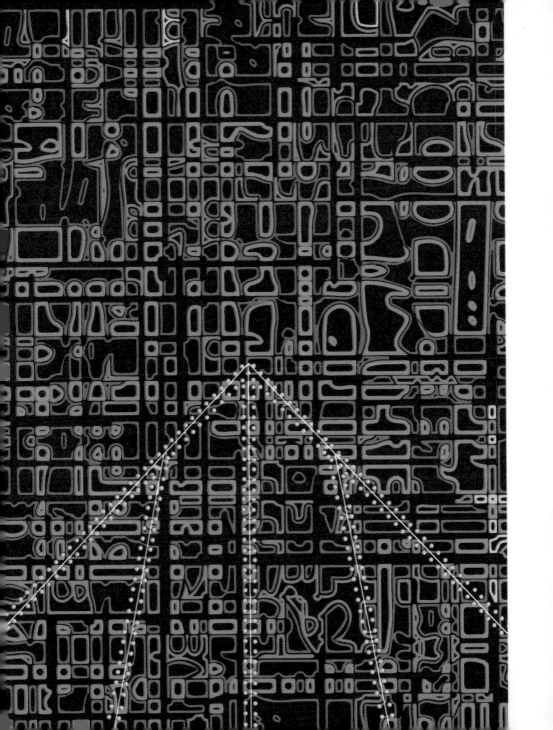

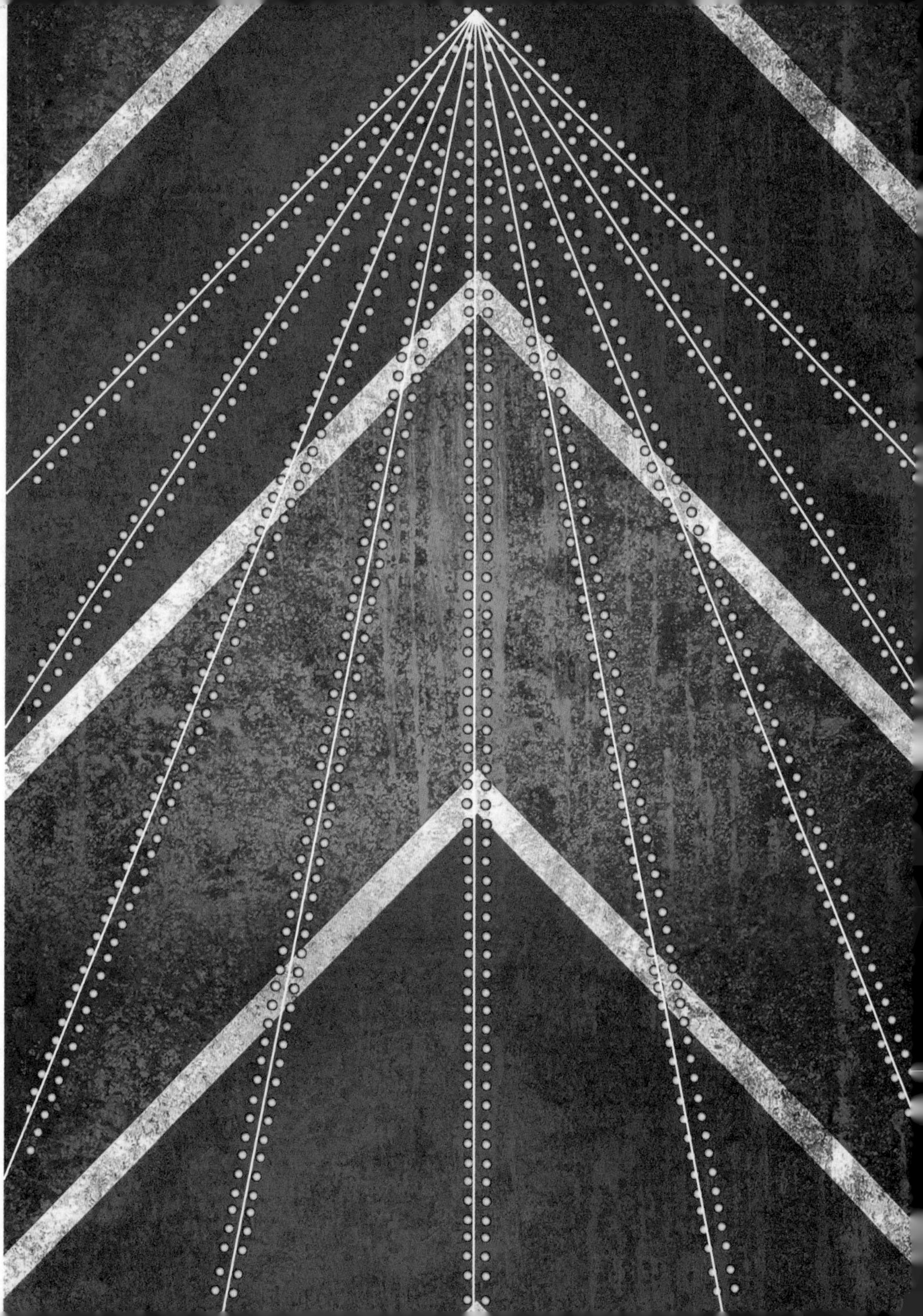

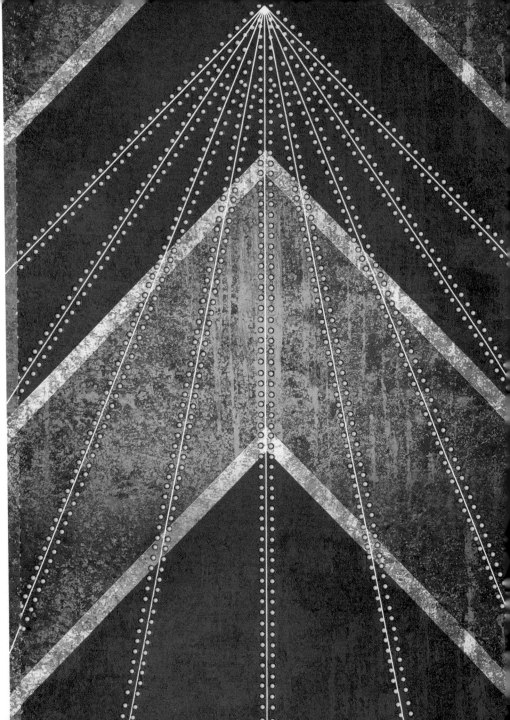

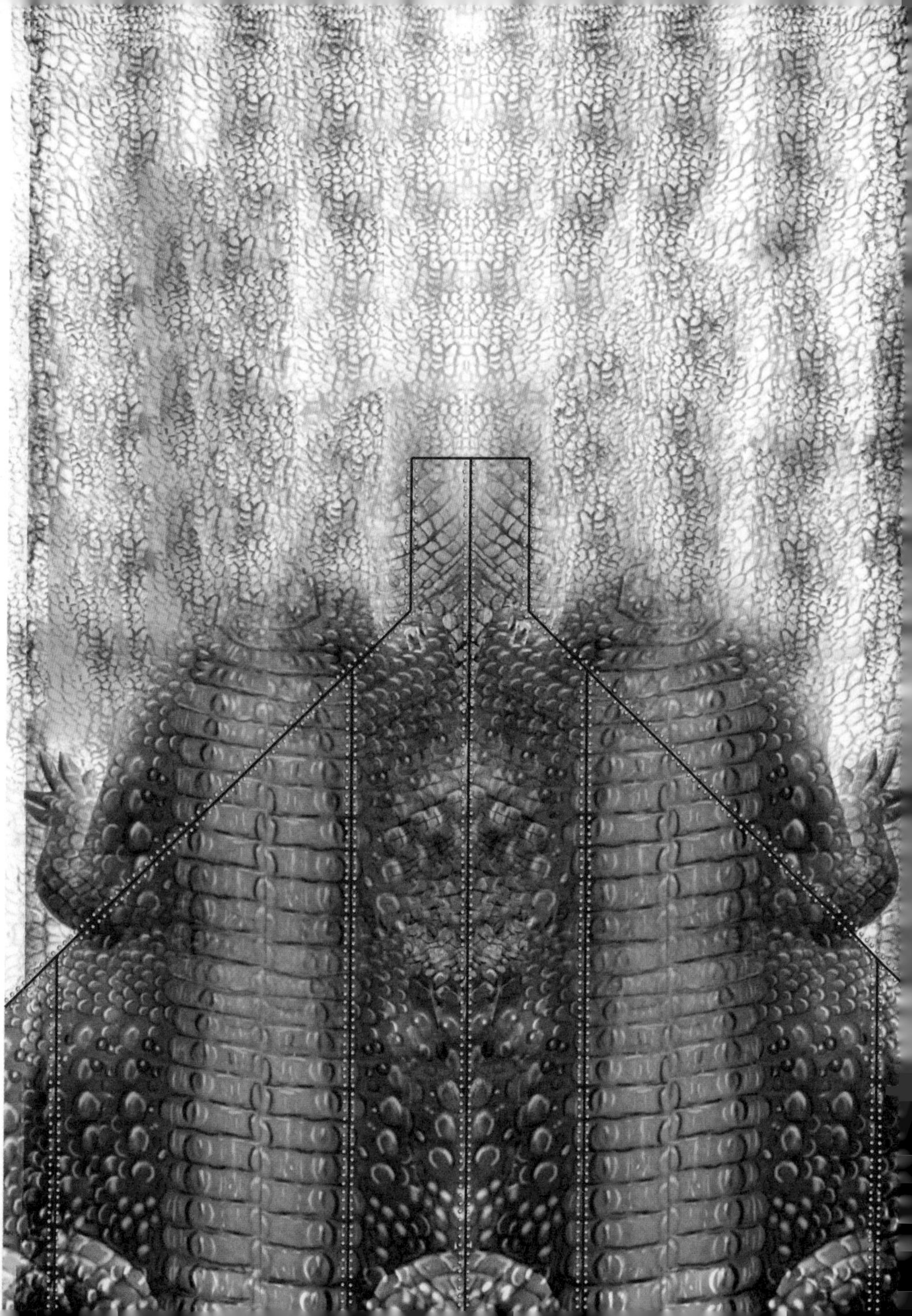

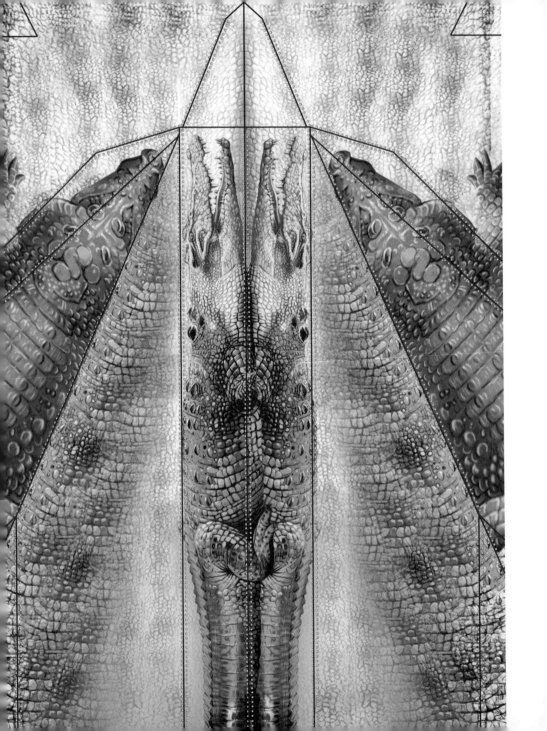

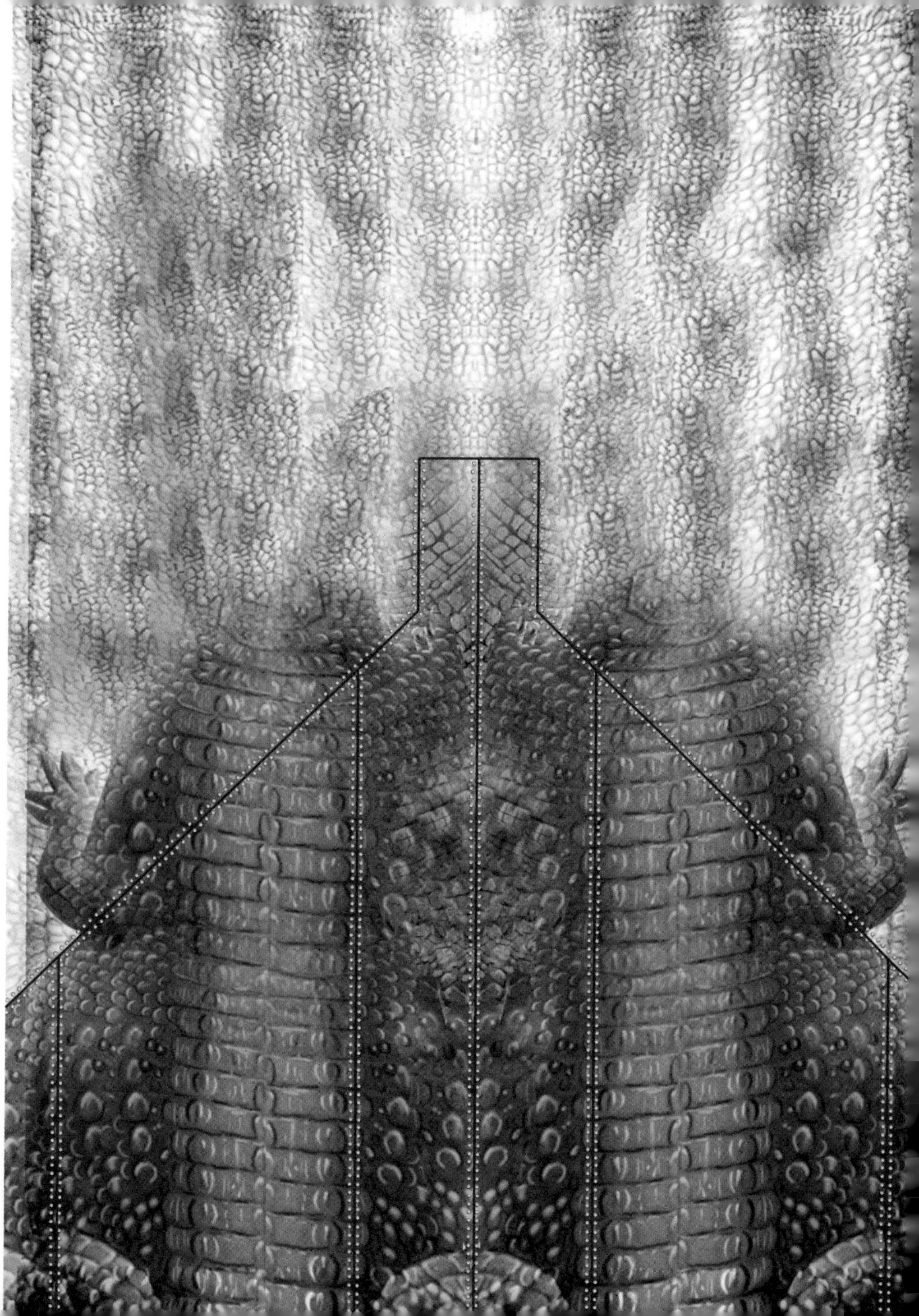

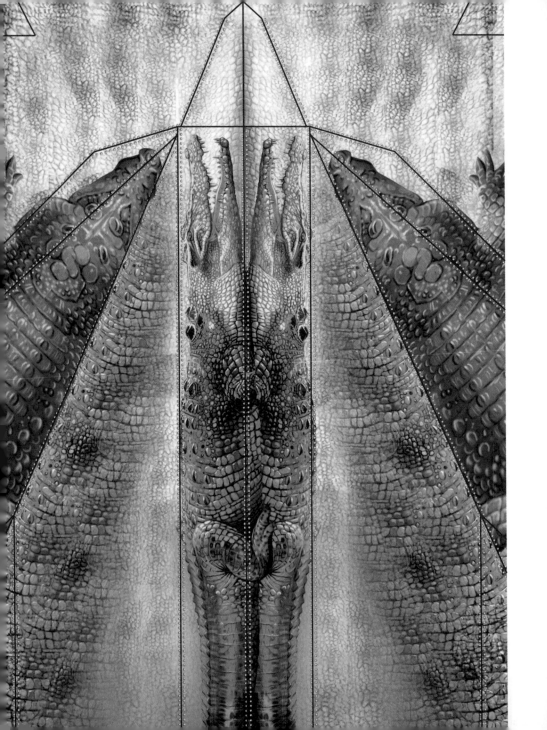

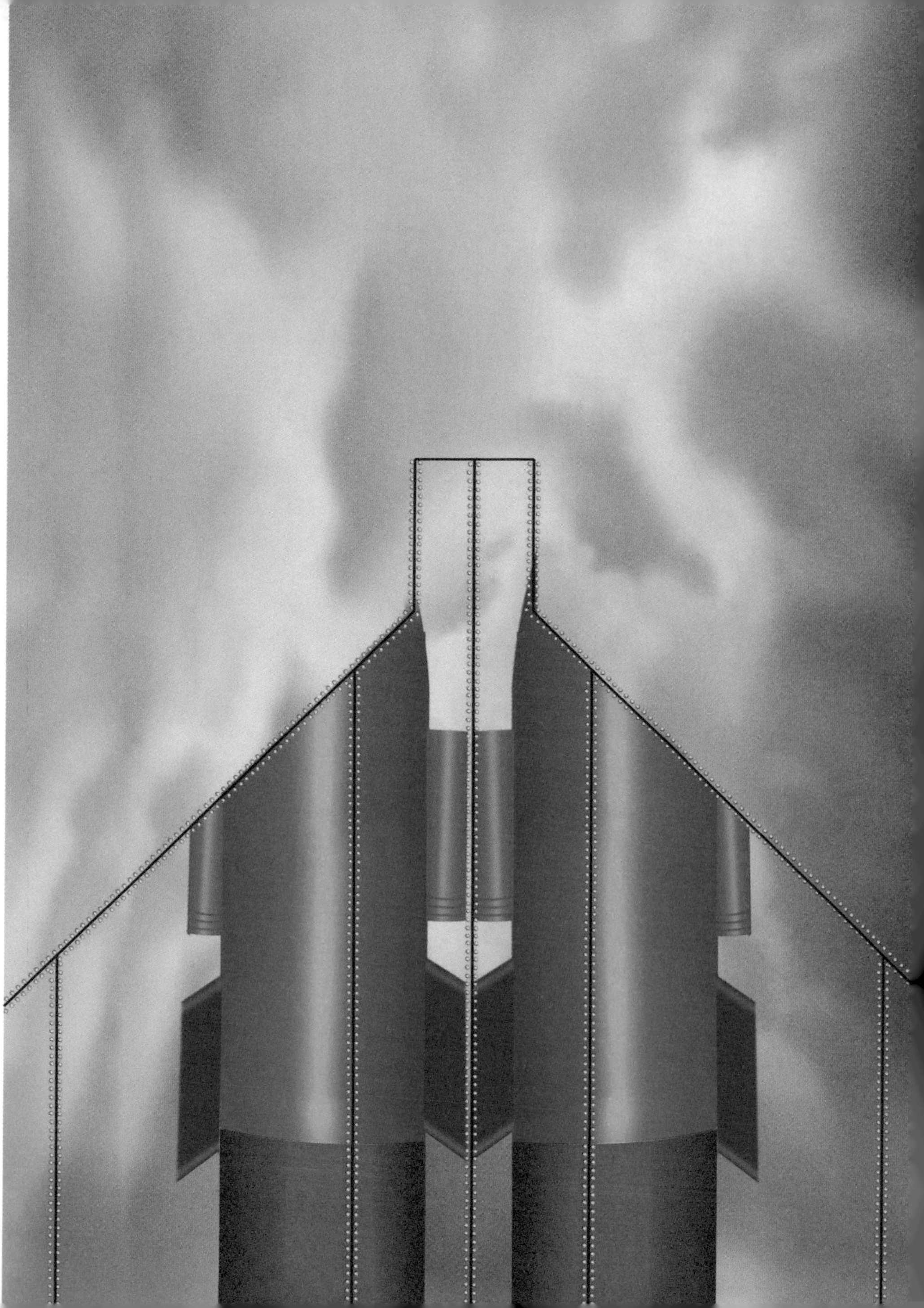

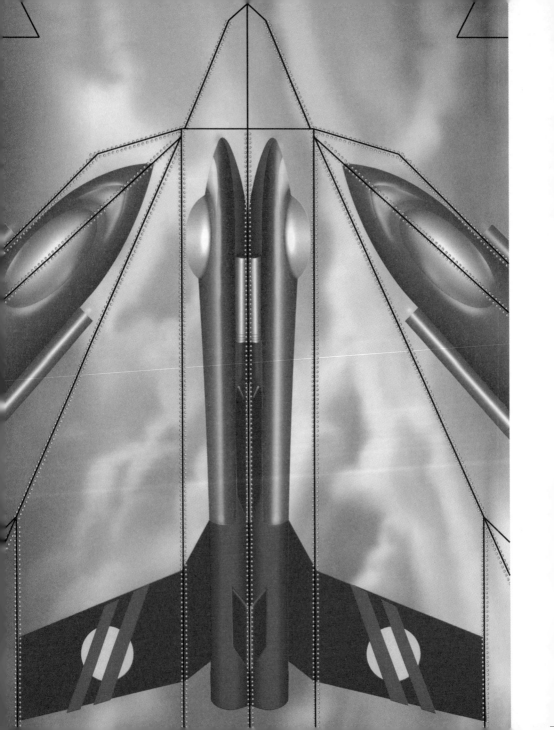

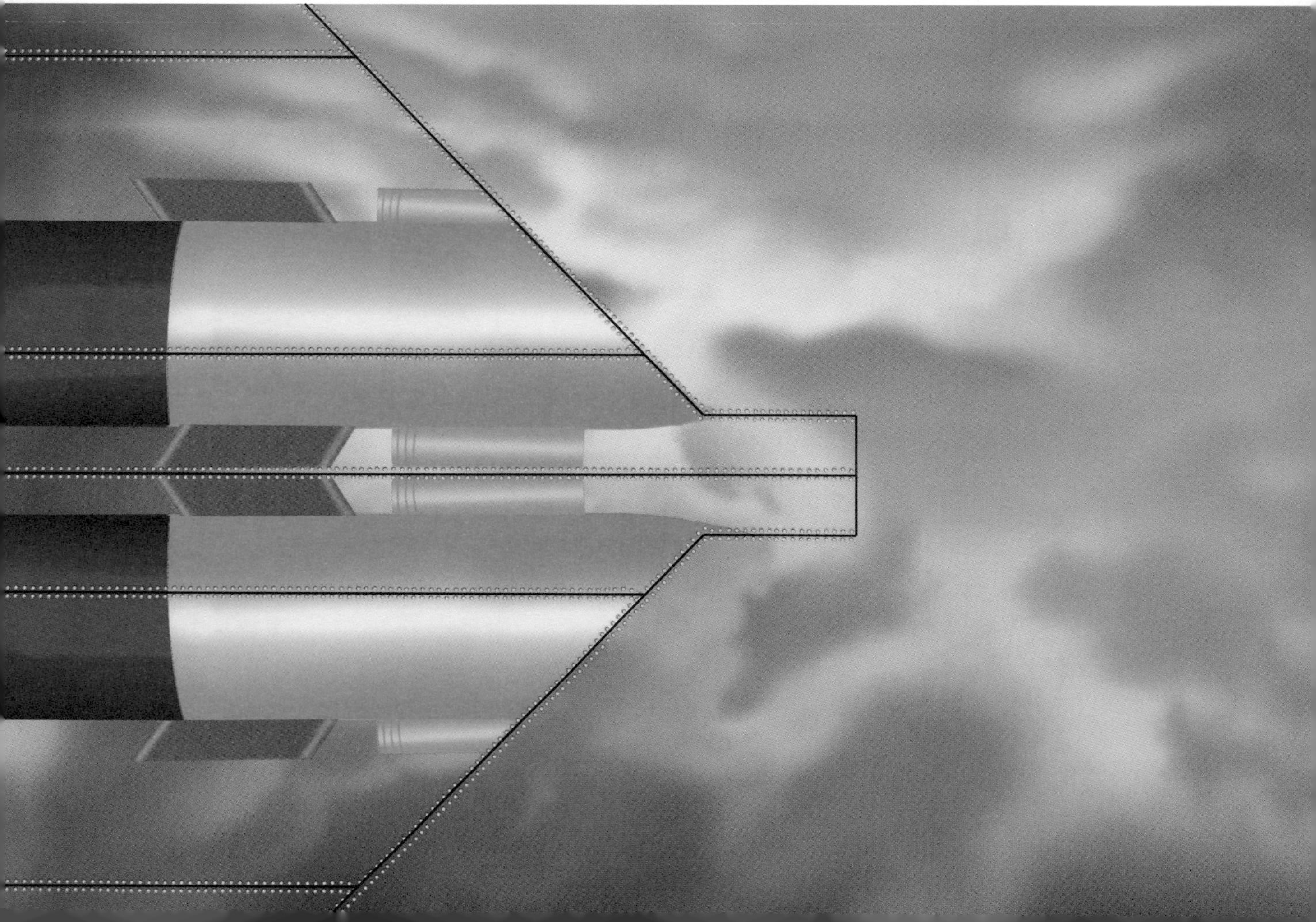

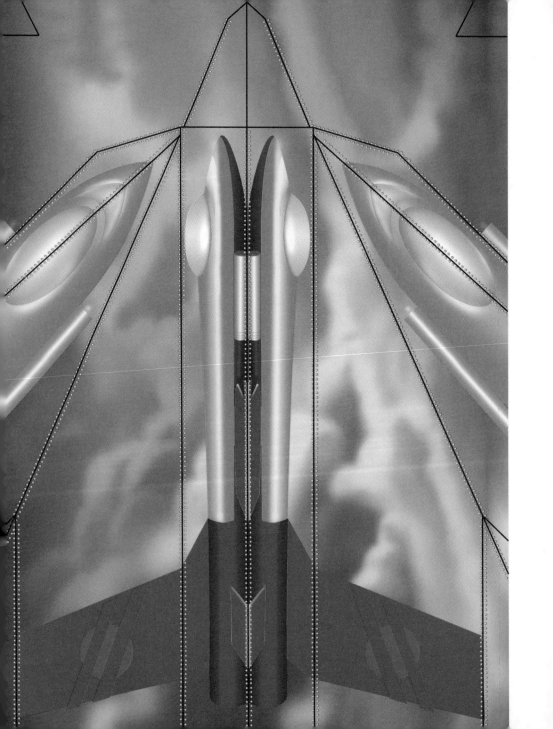

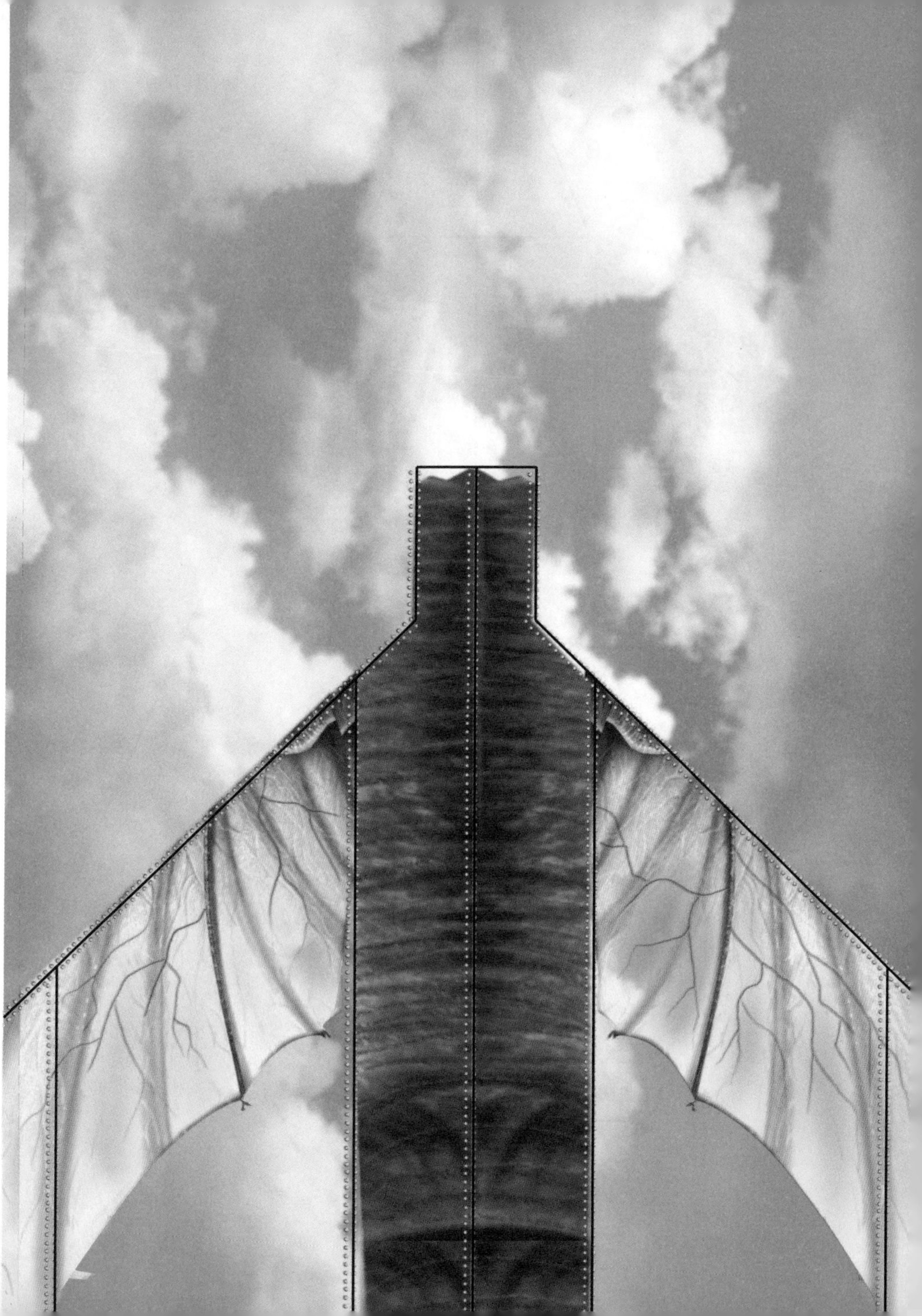

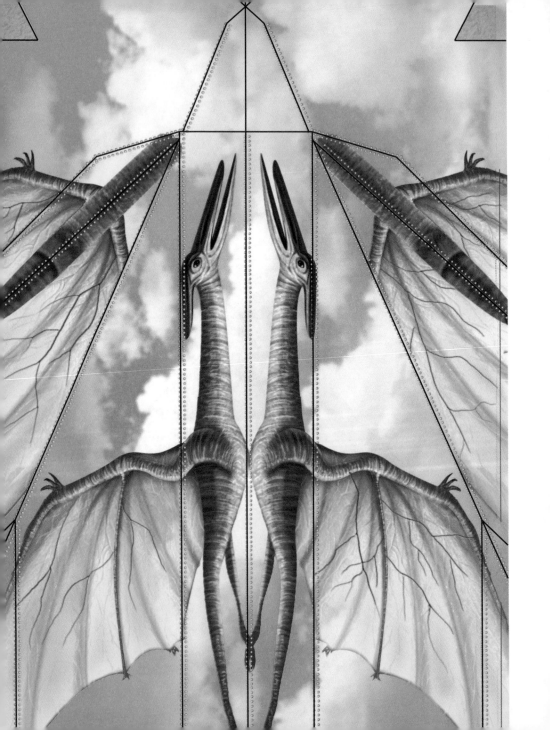

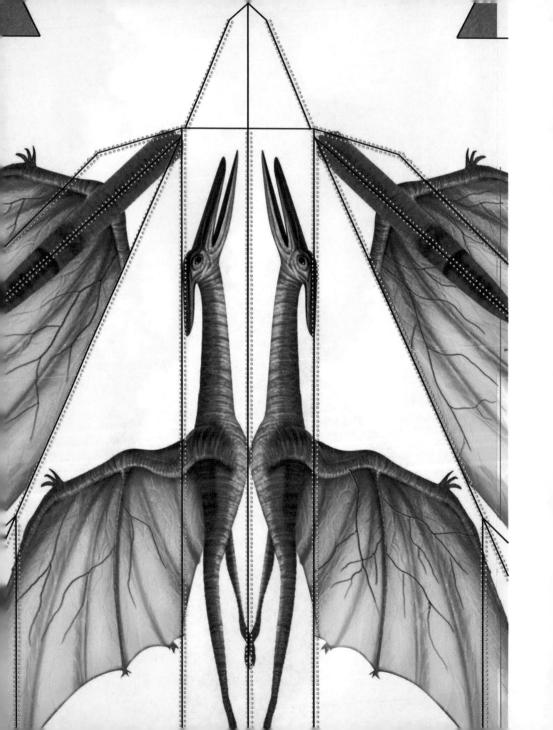

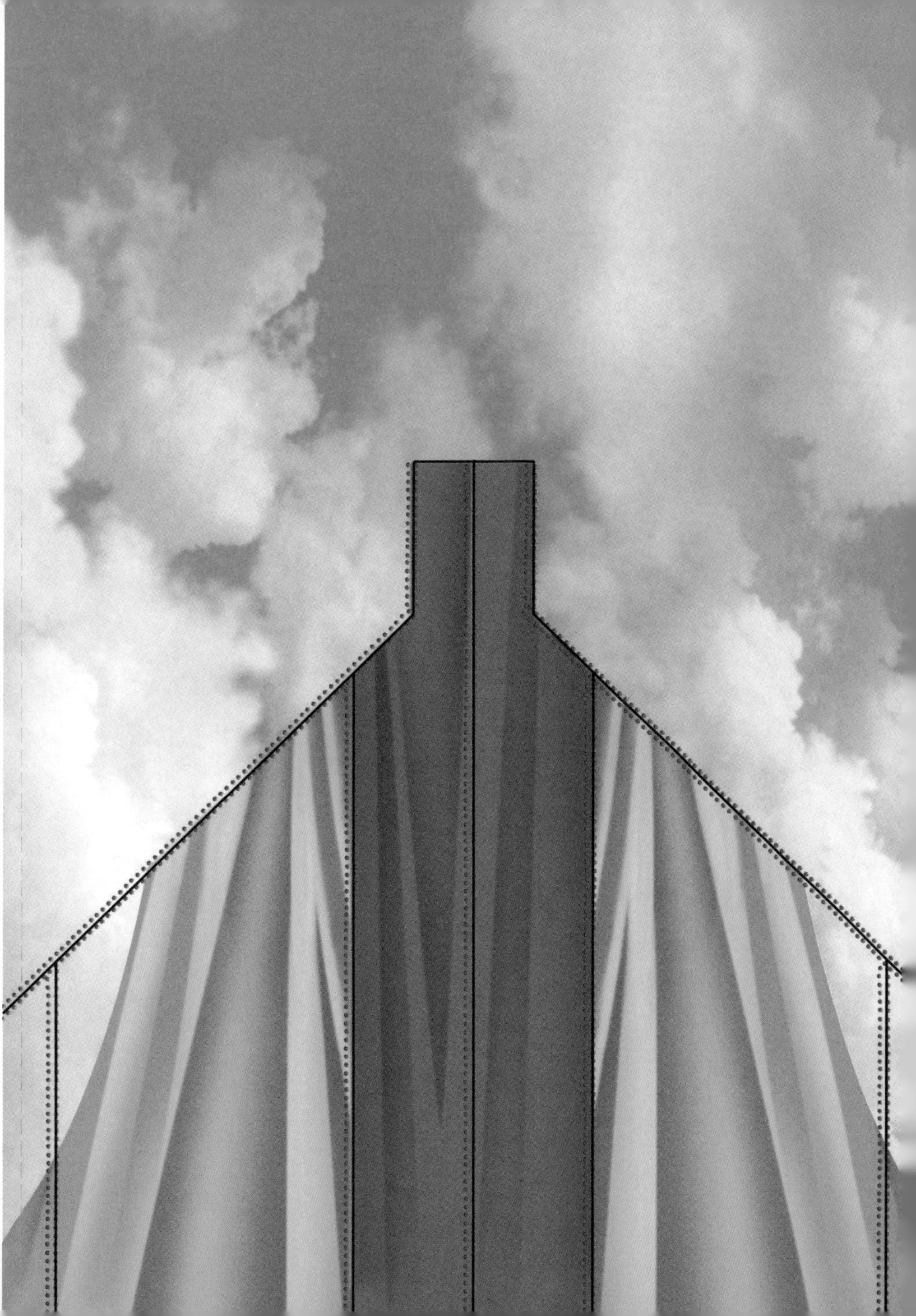

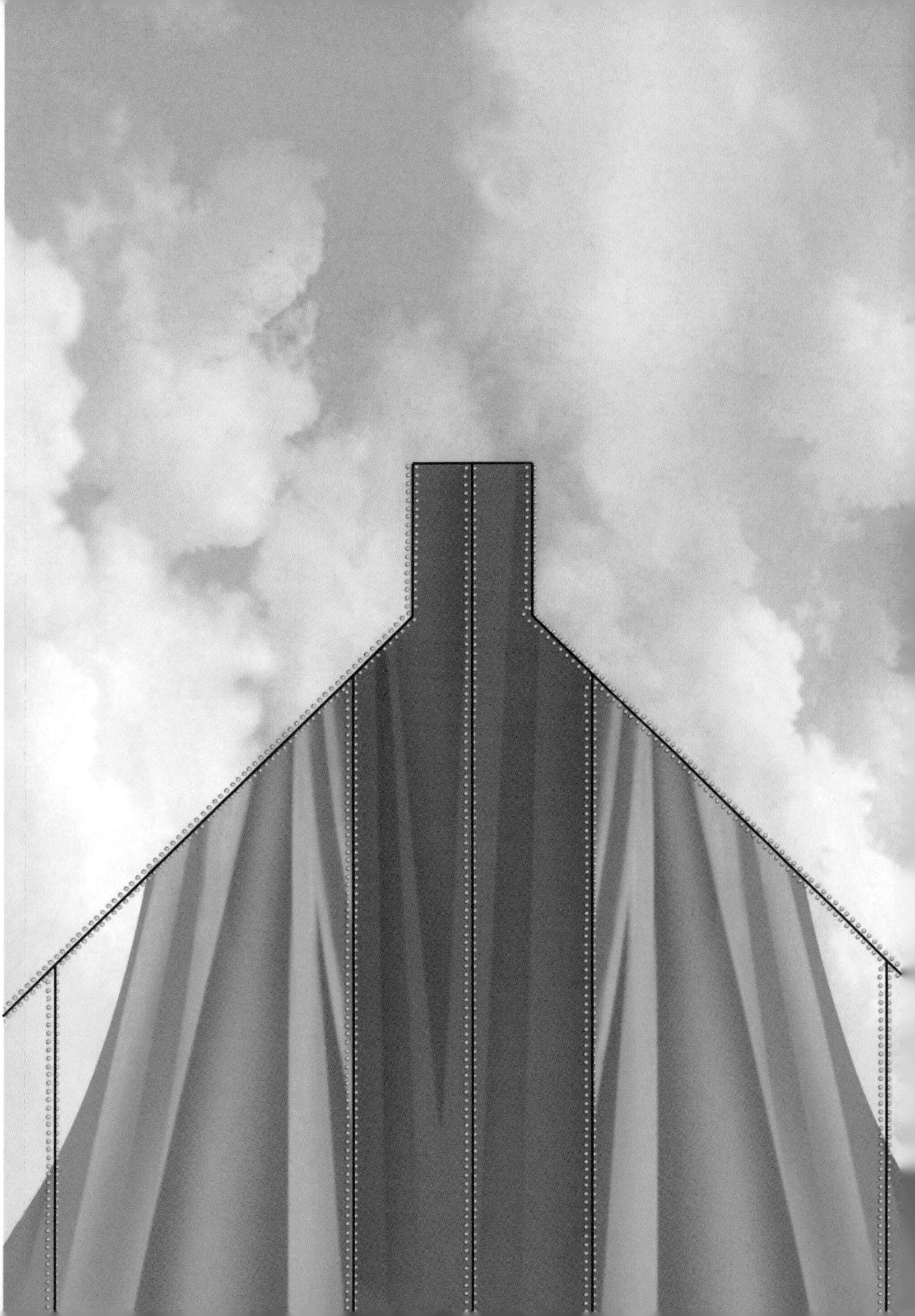

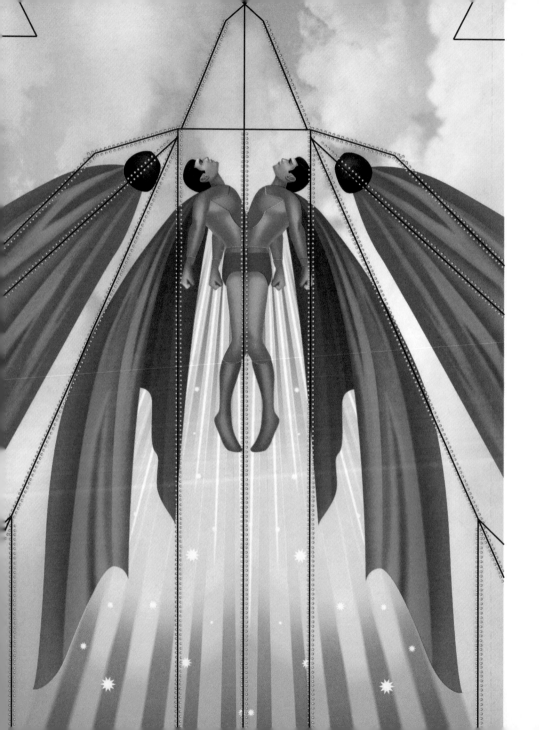

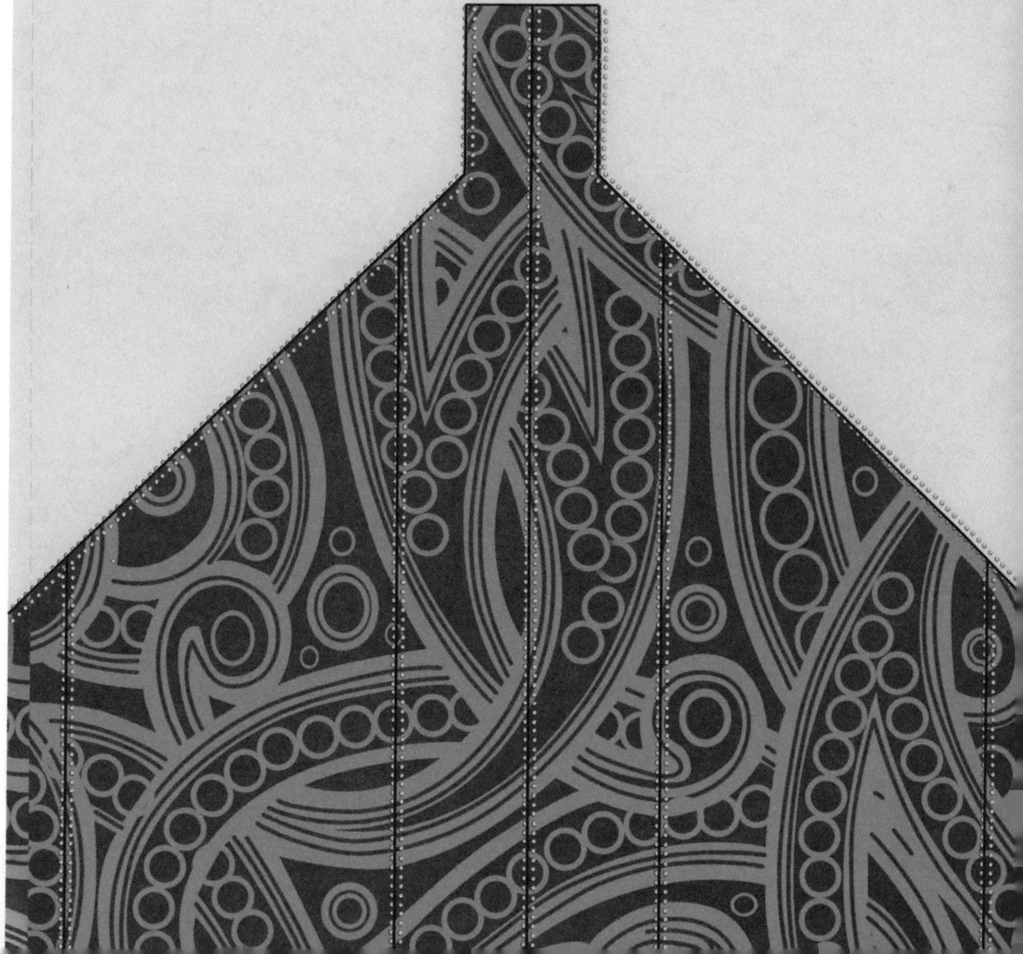

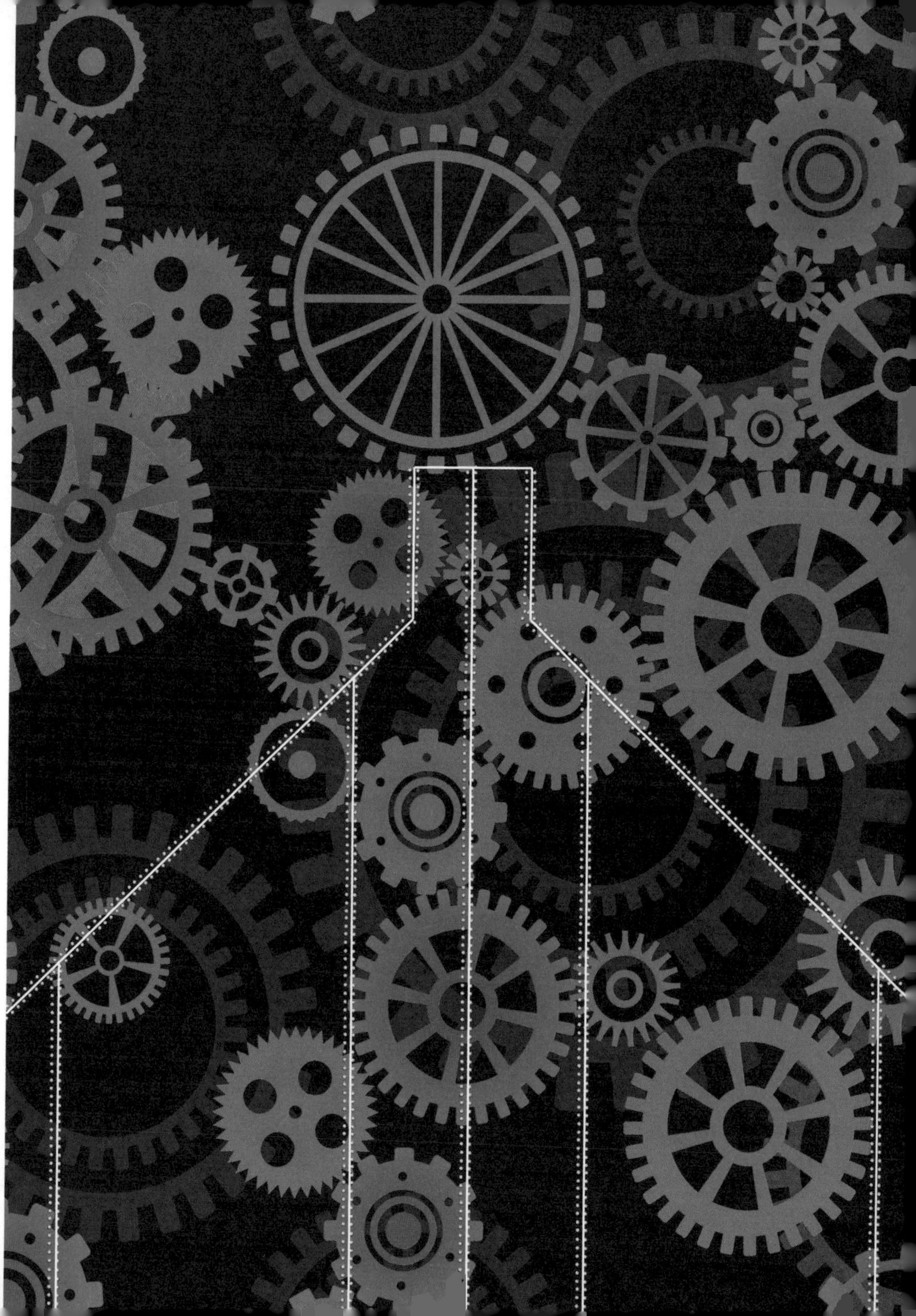

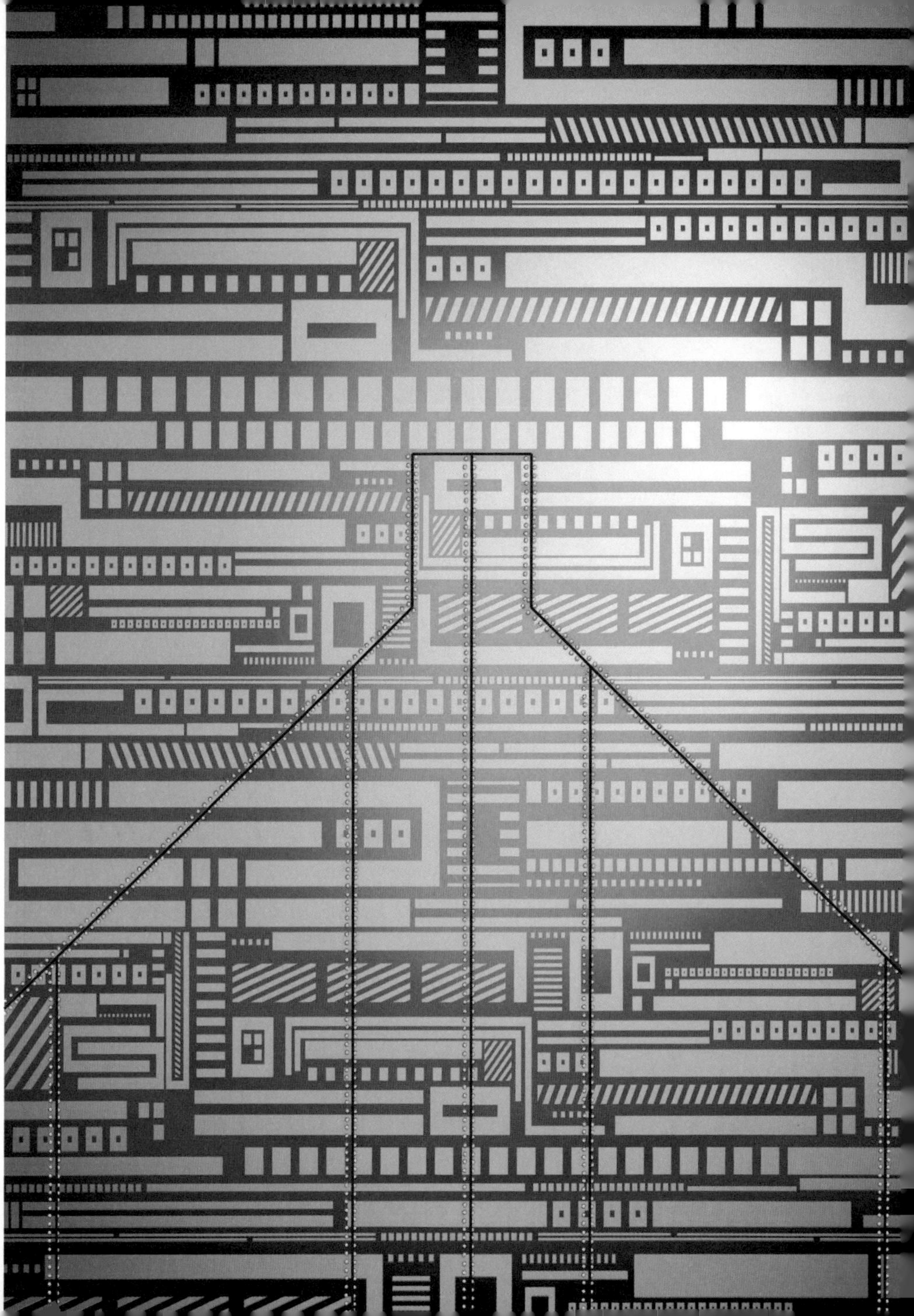

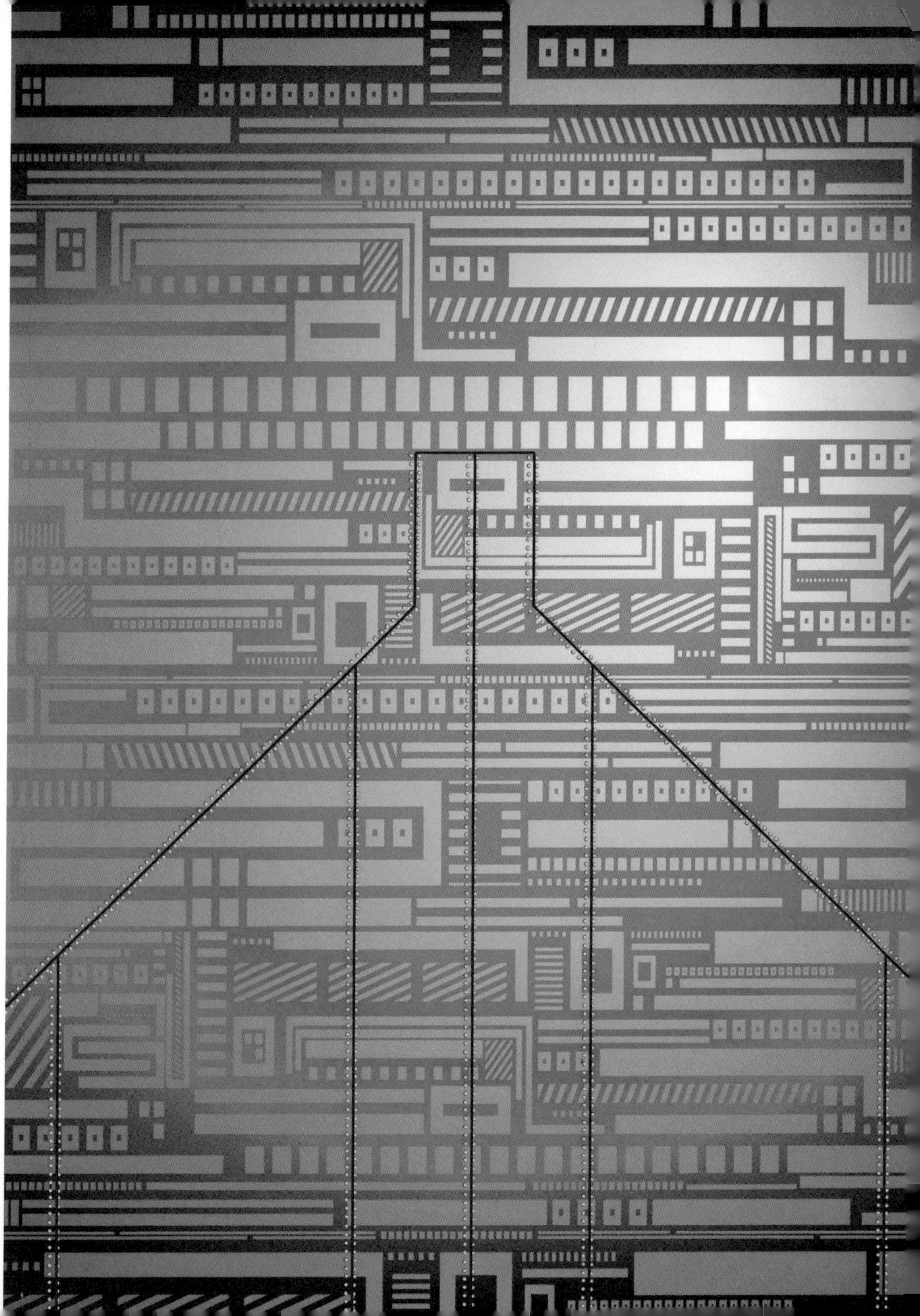

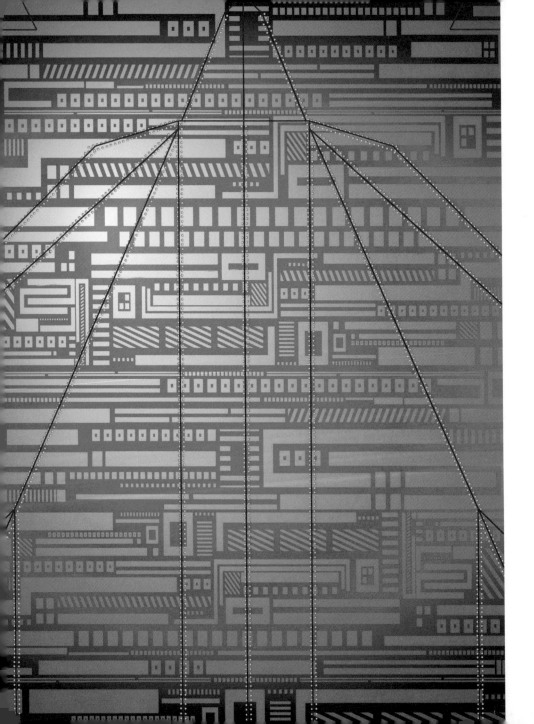

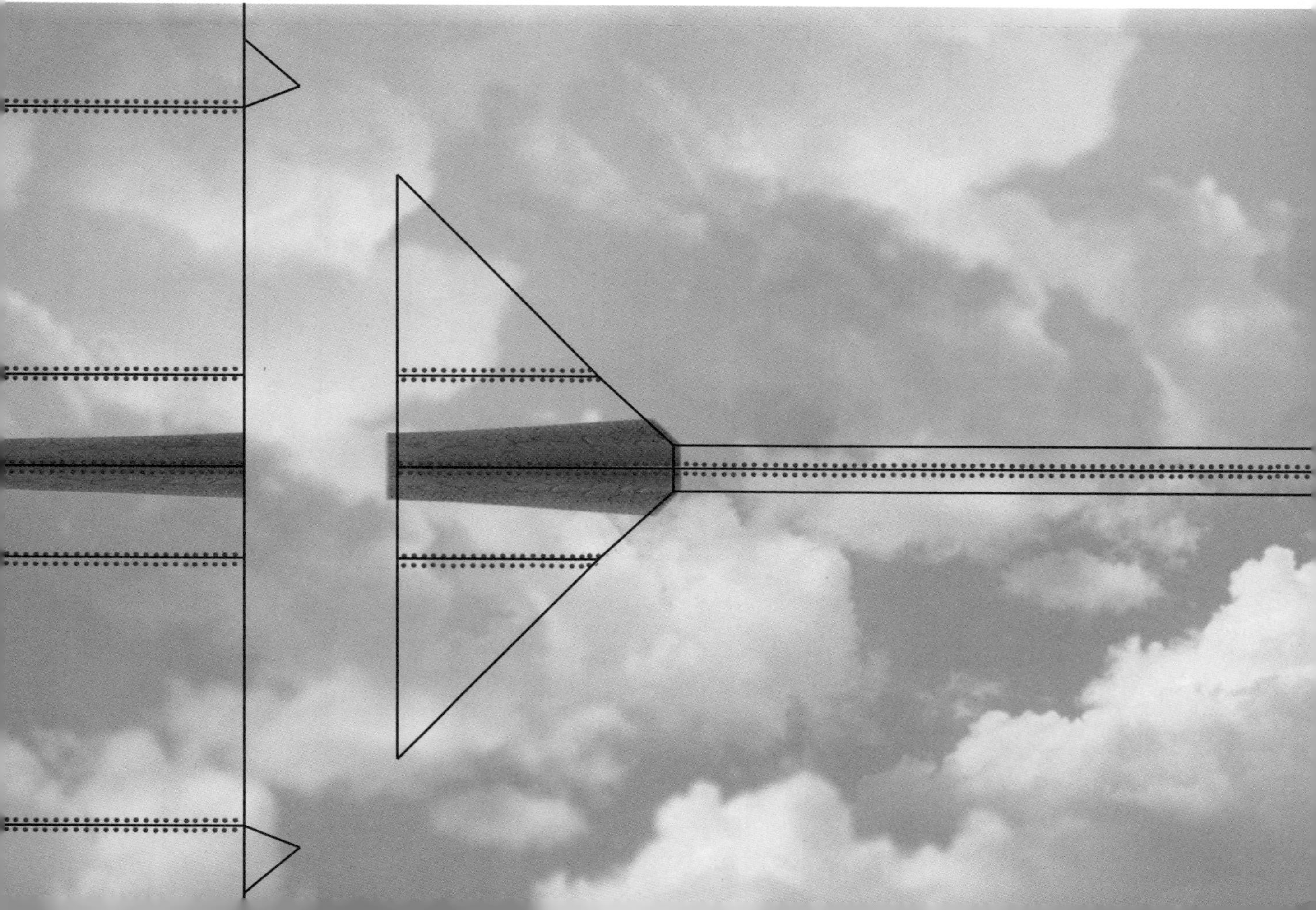

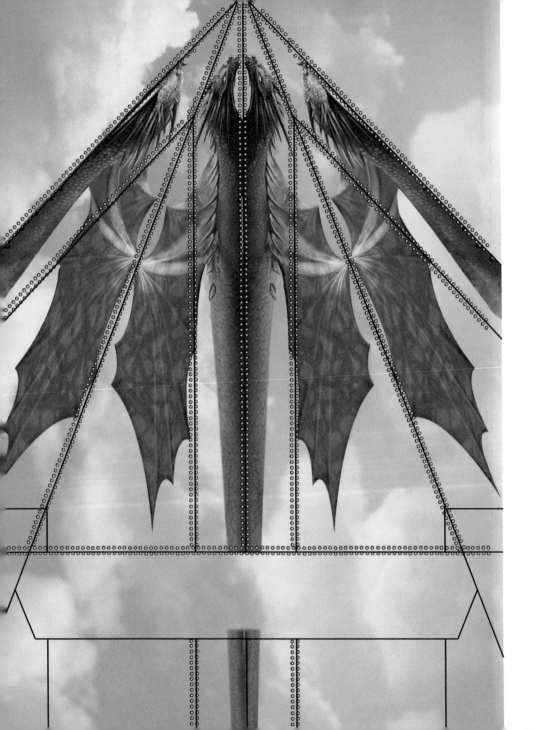

AFTERBURNER

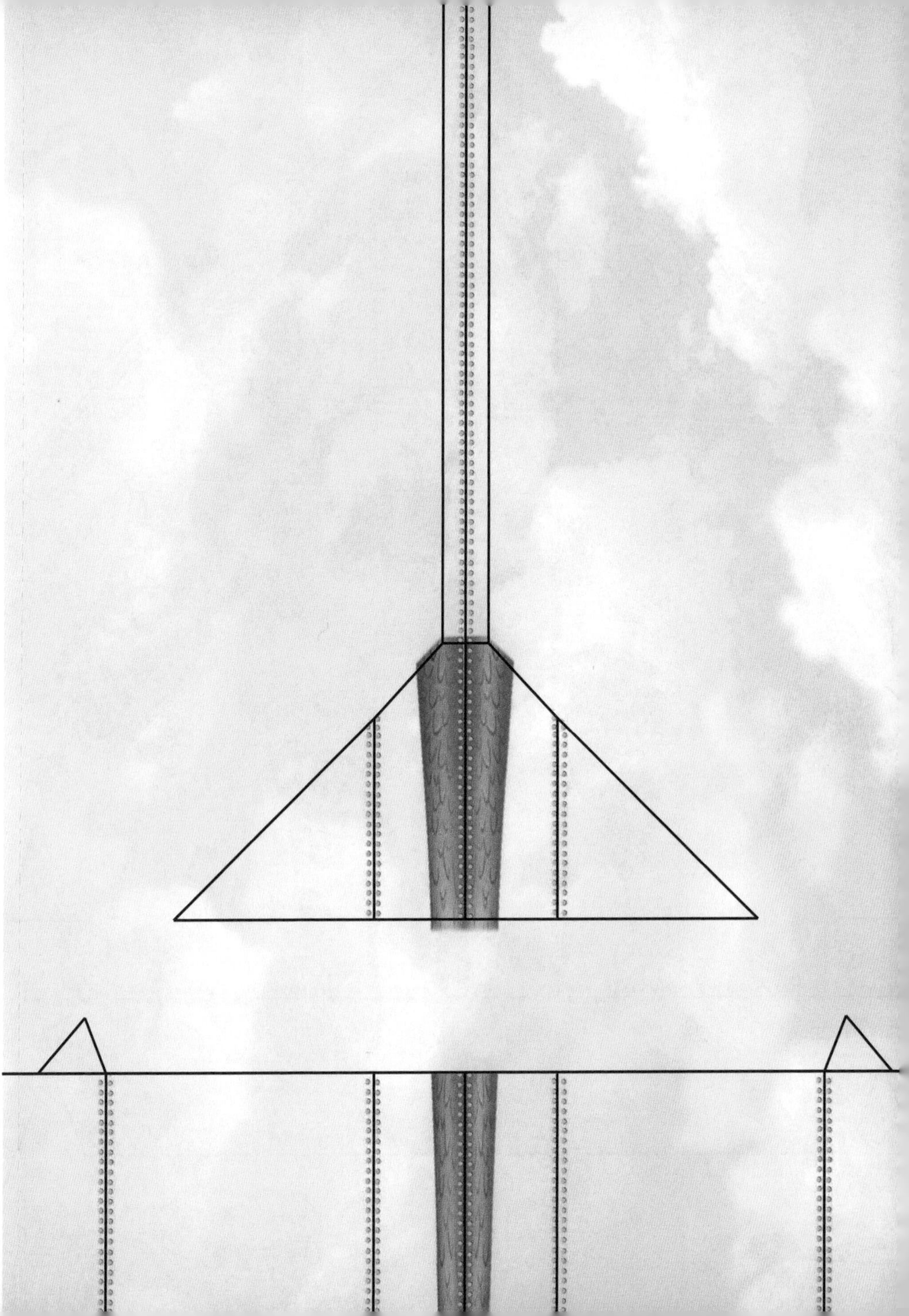

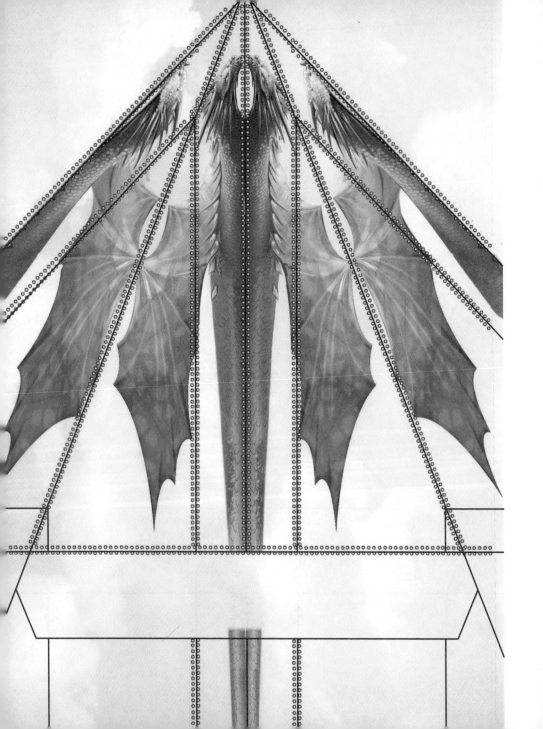

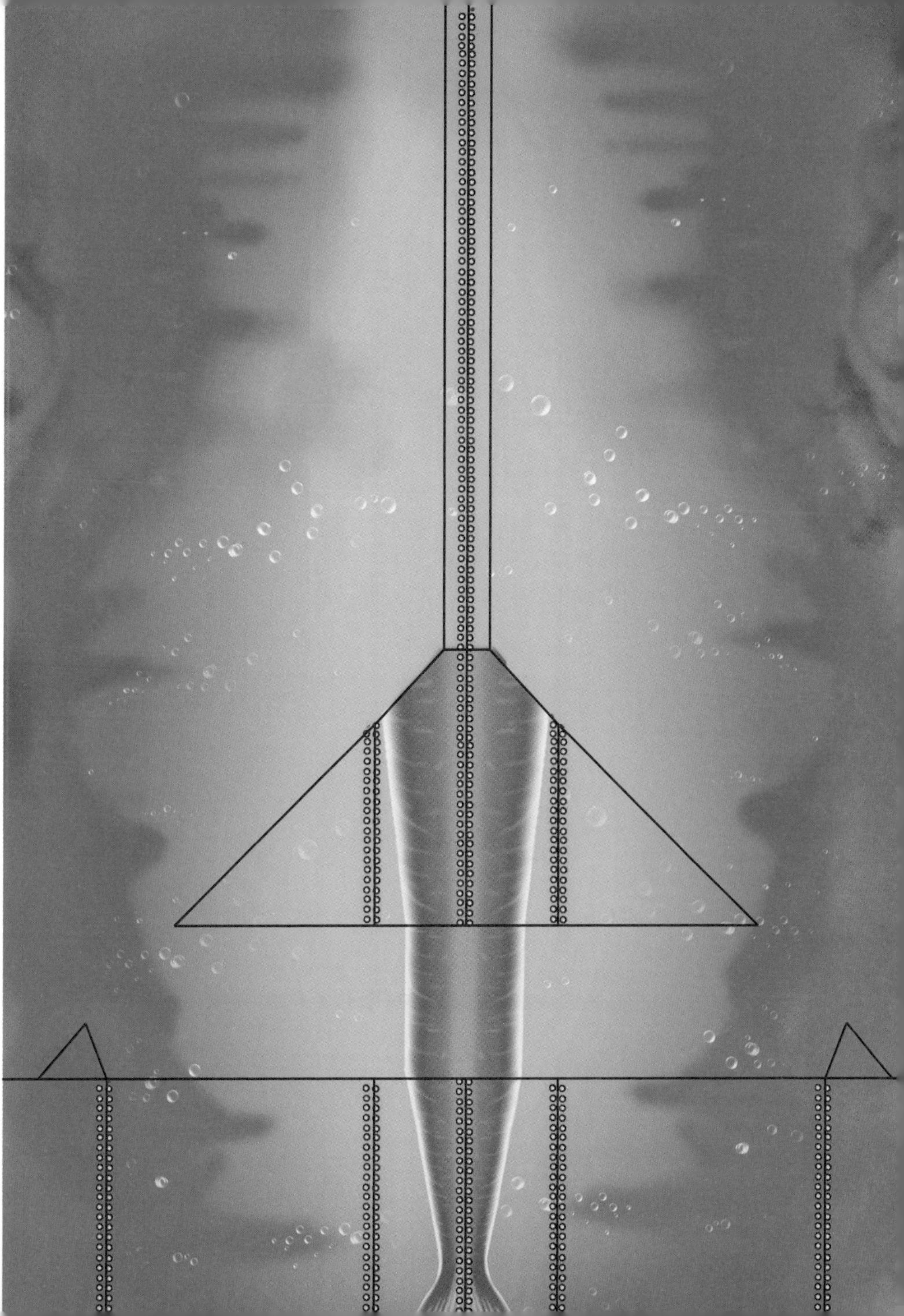

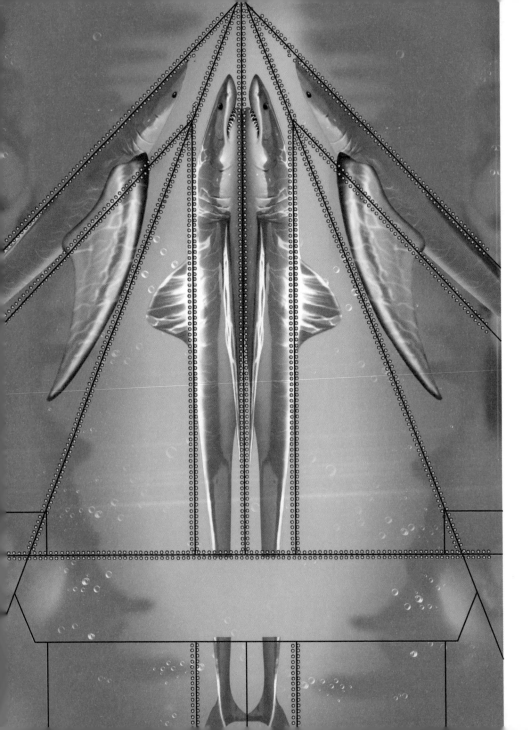

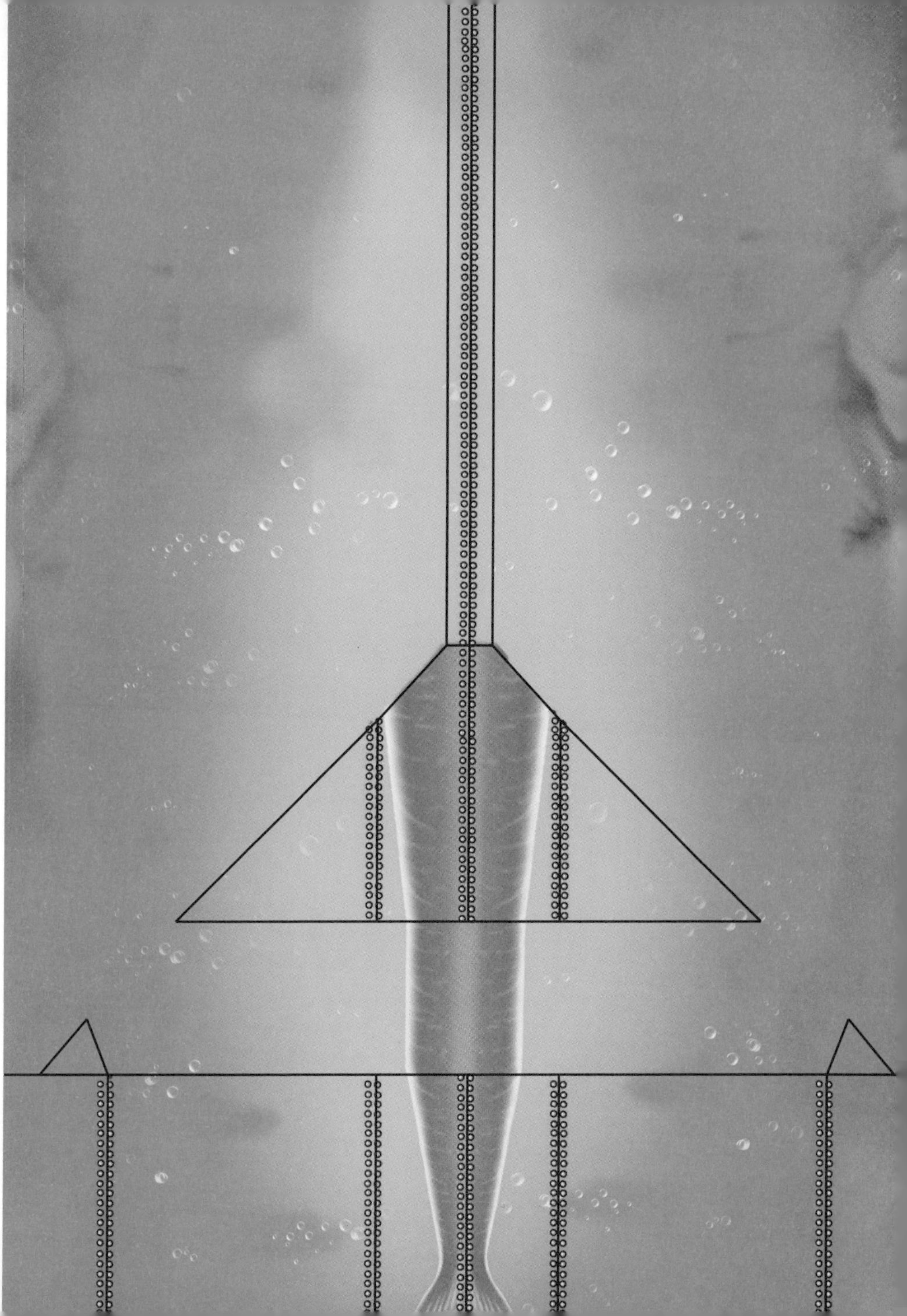

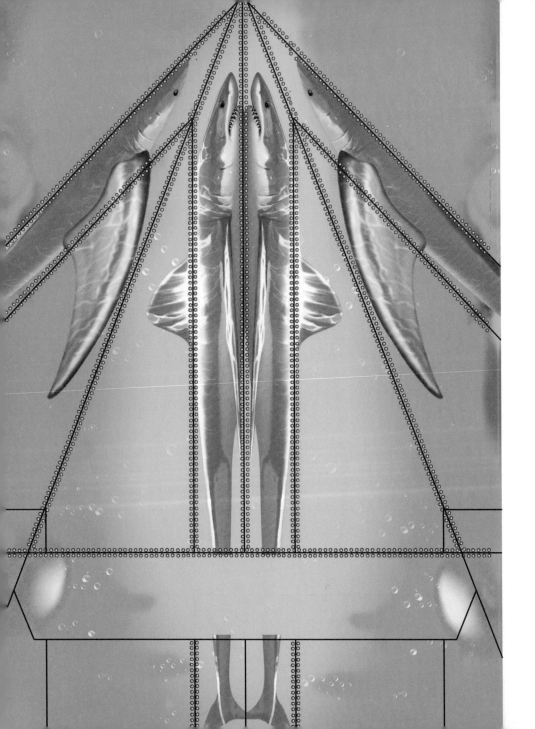

AFTERBURNER

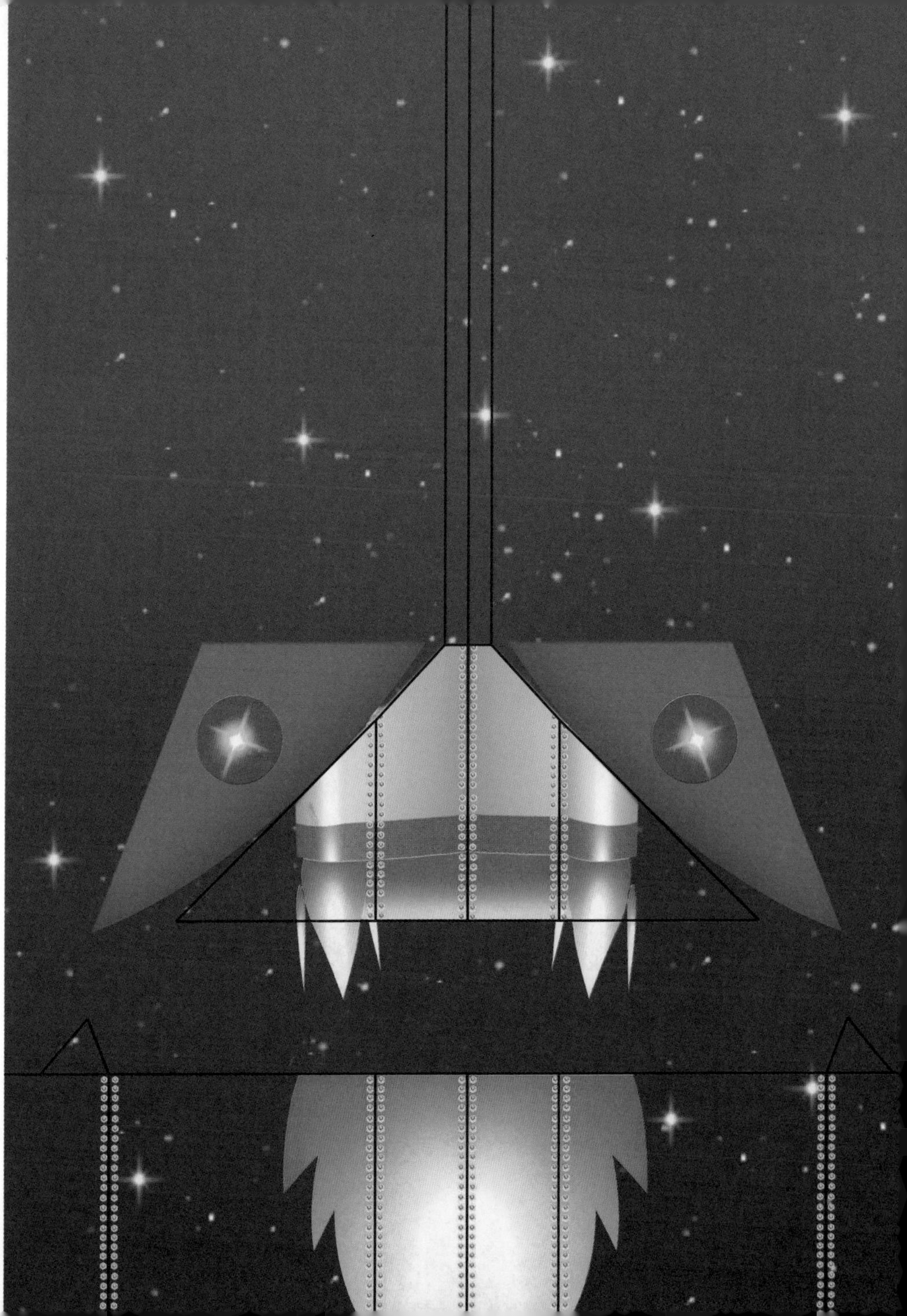

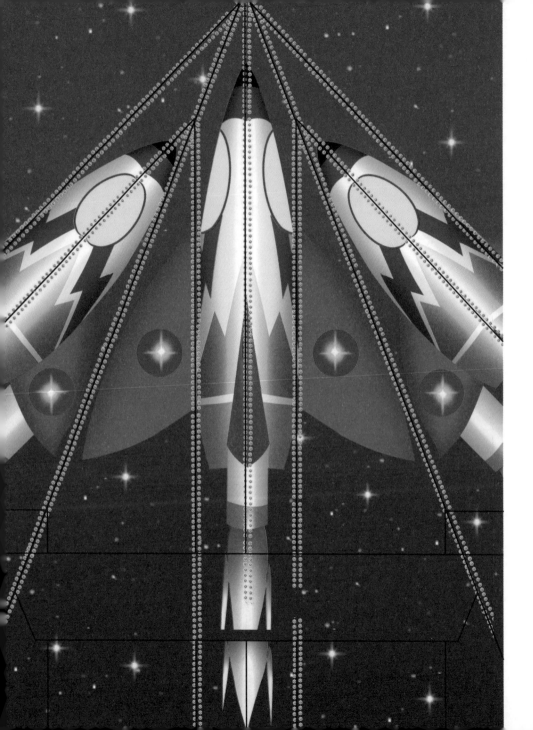

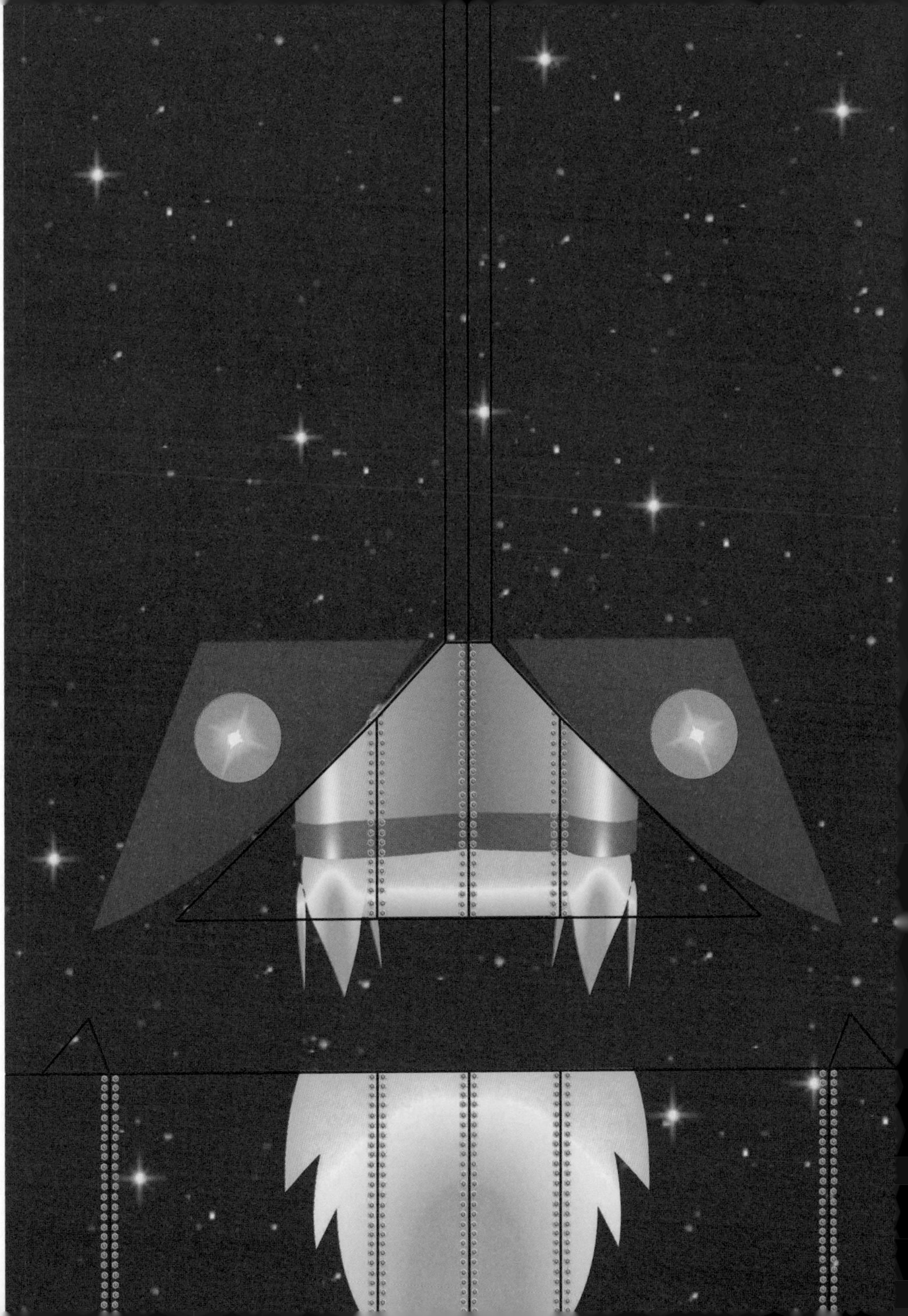

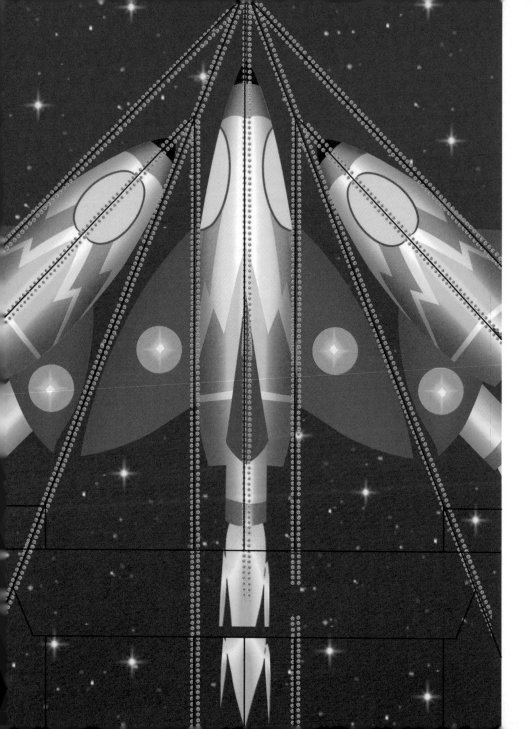

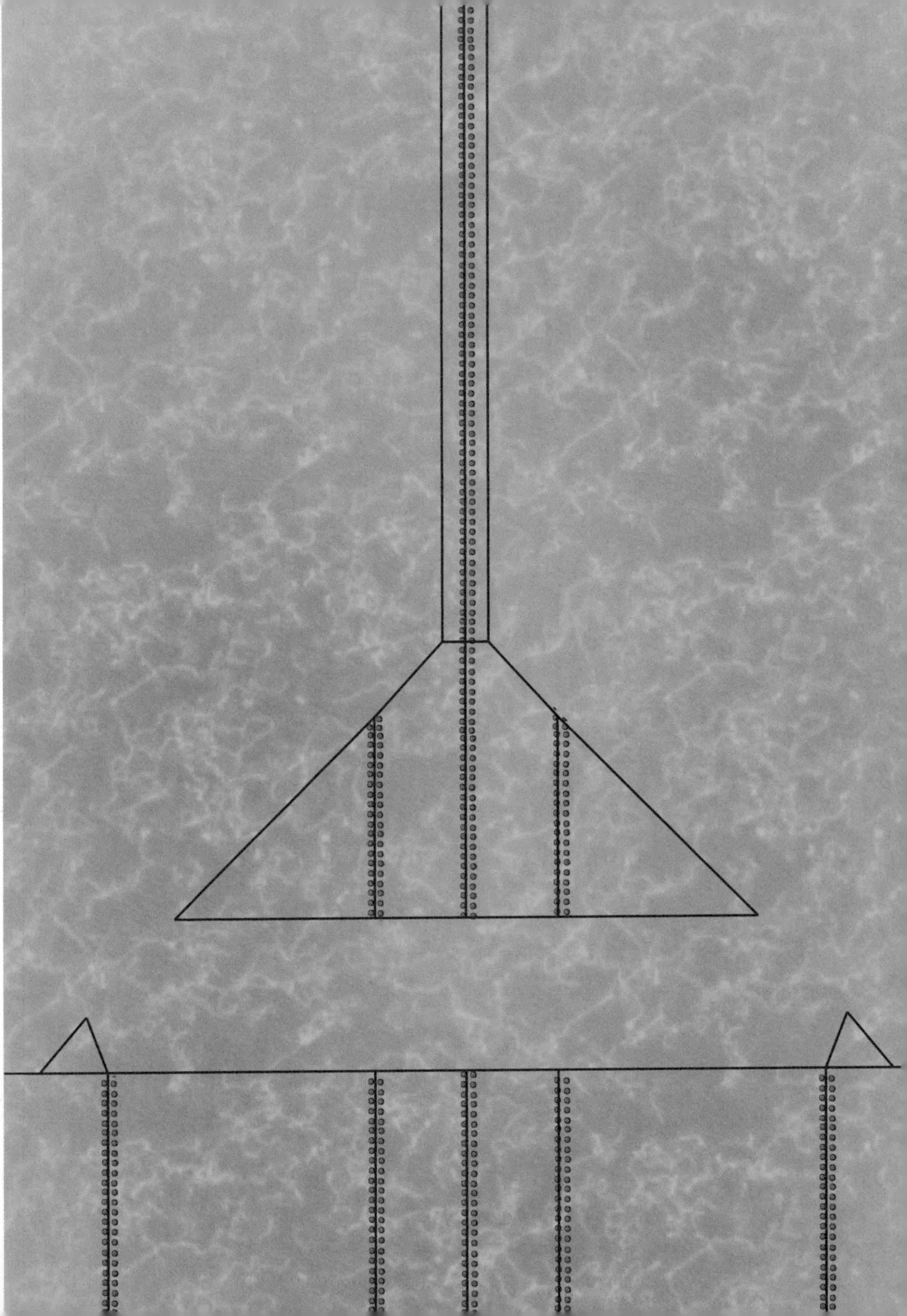

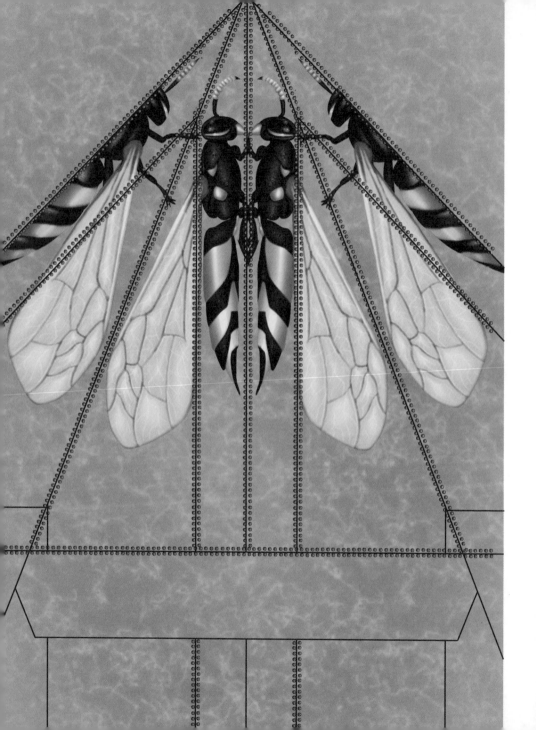

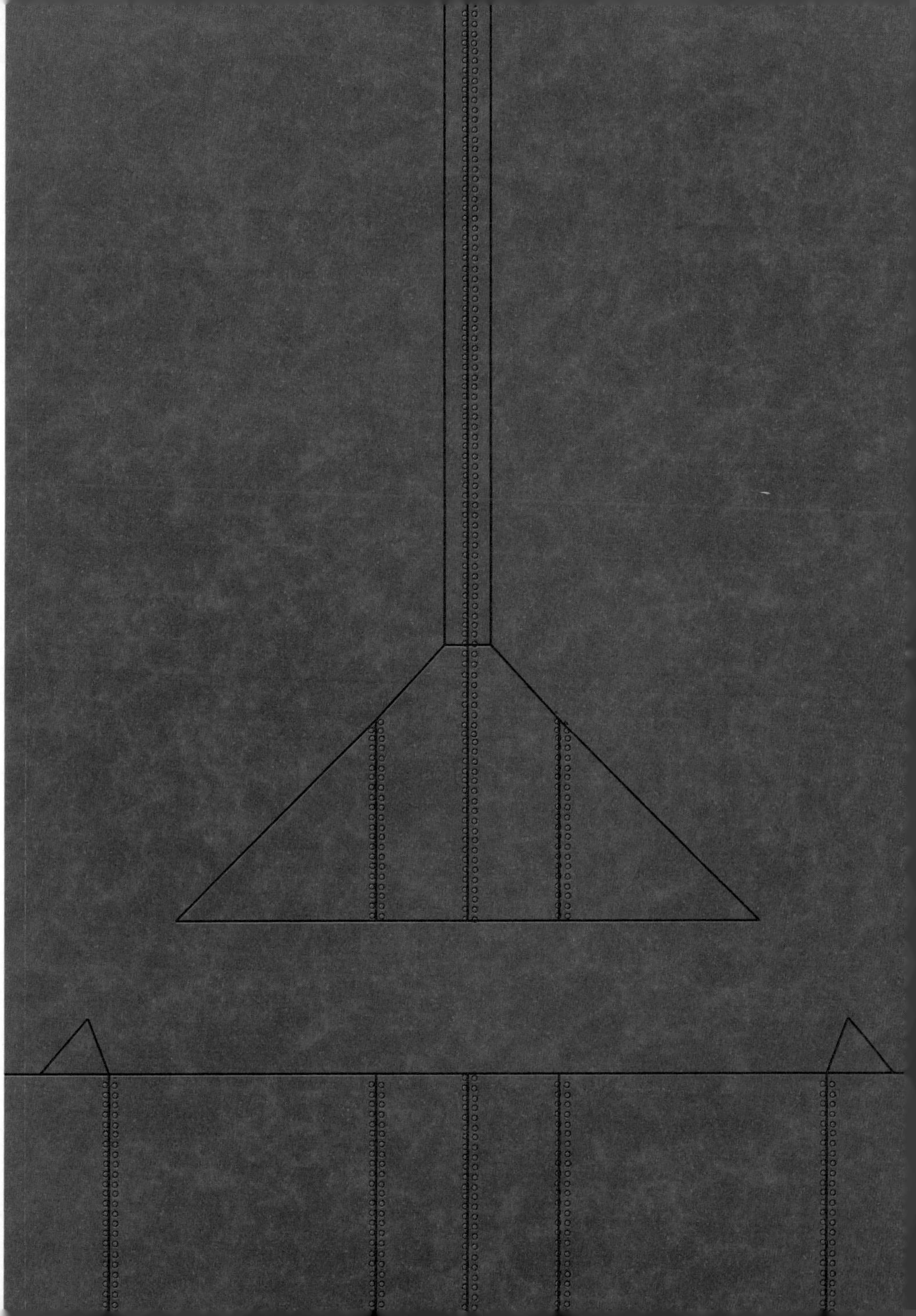

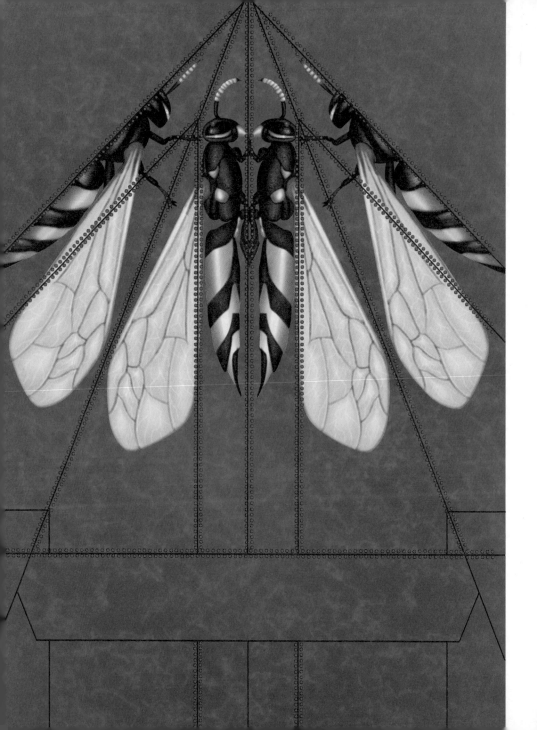

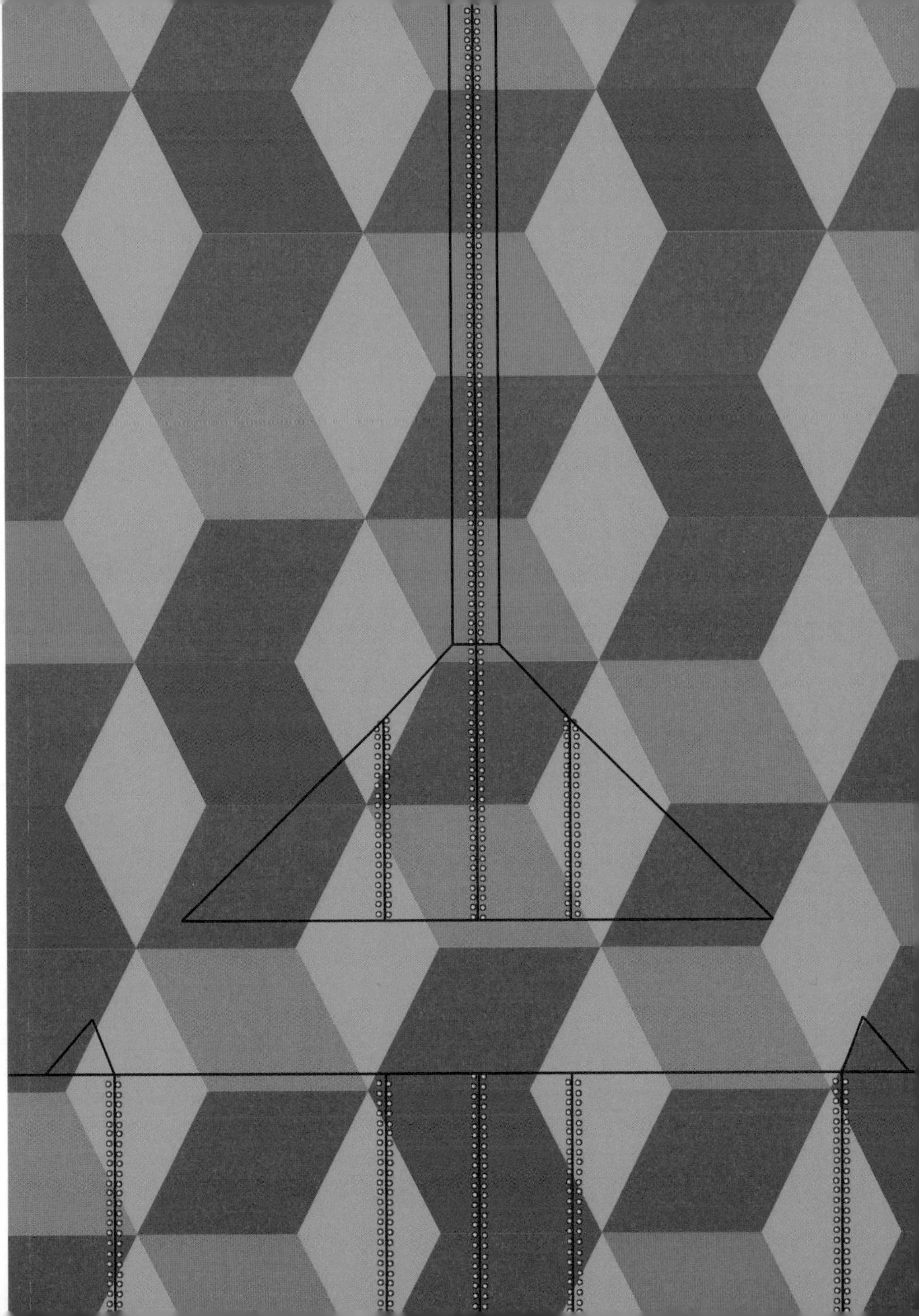

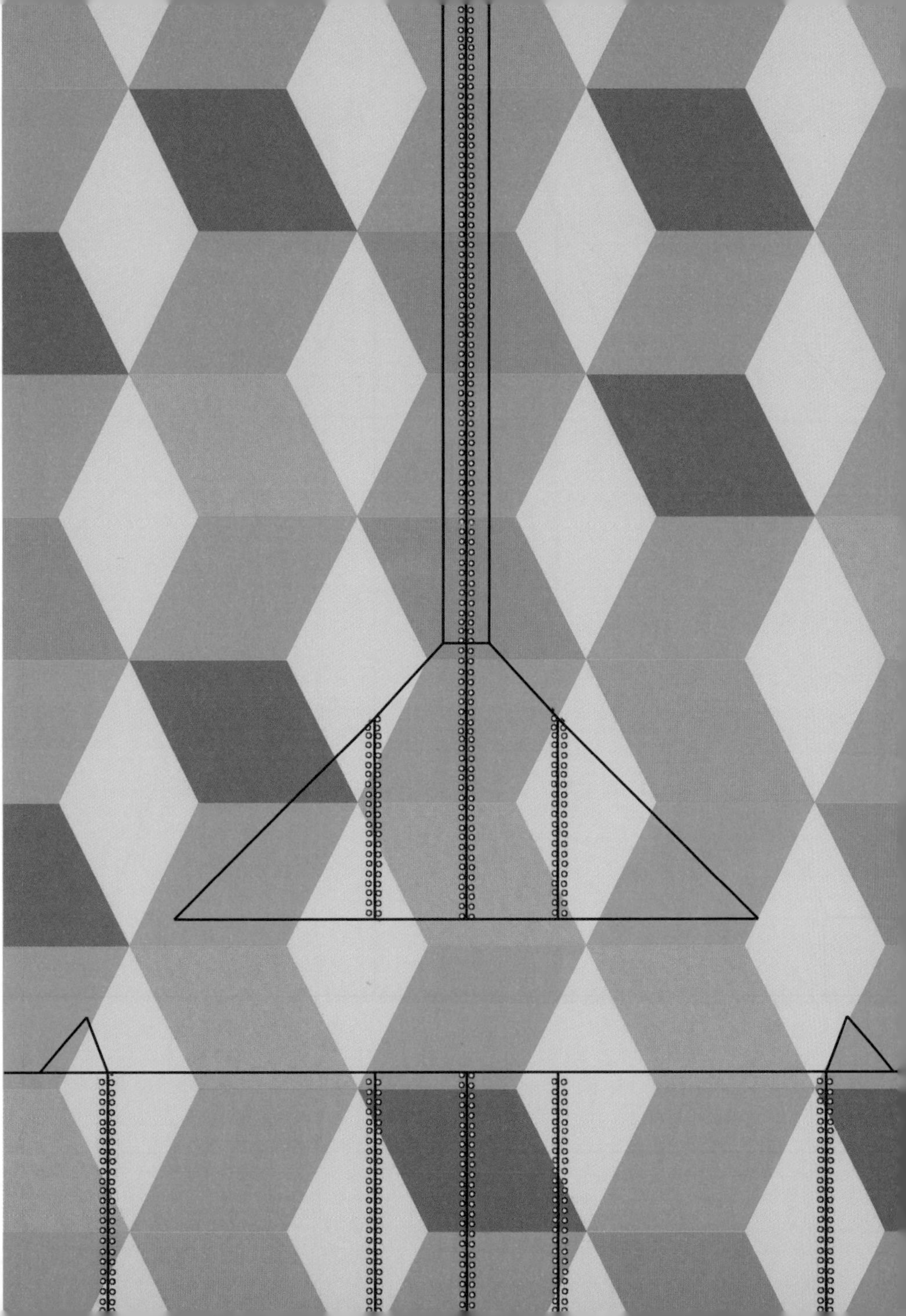

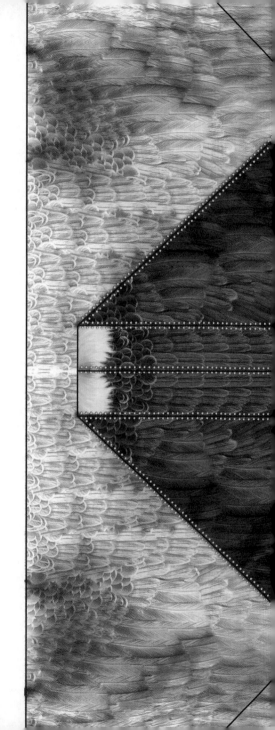

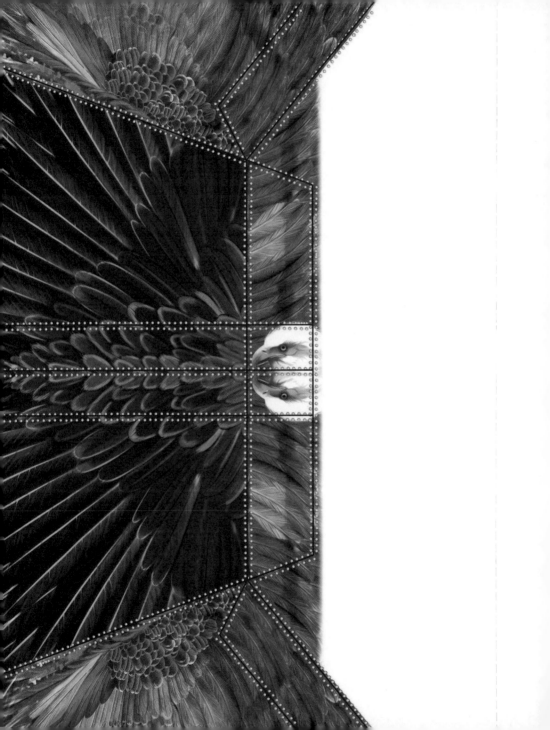

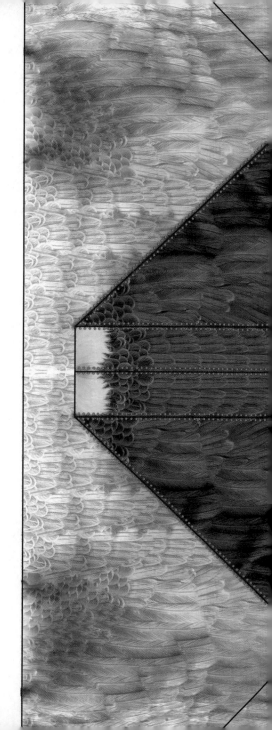

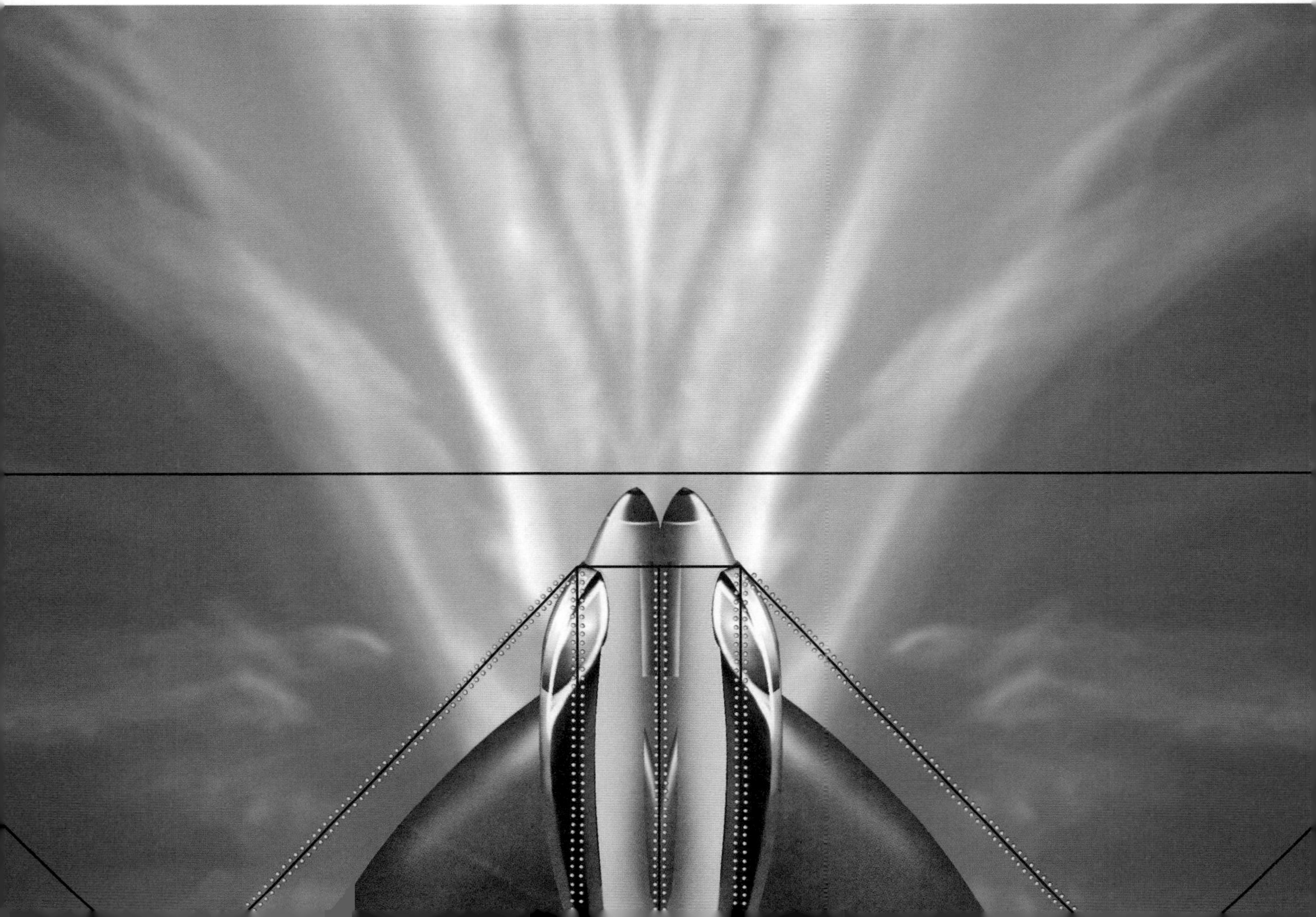

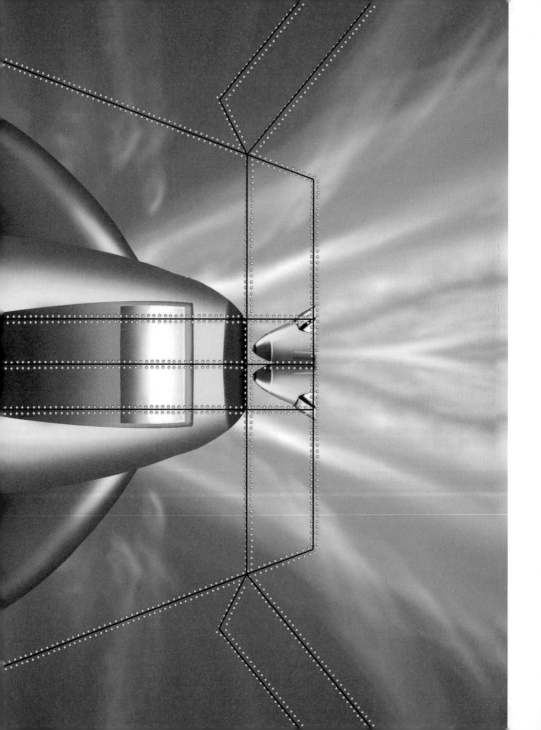

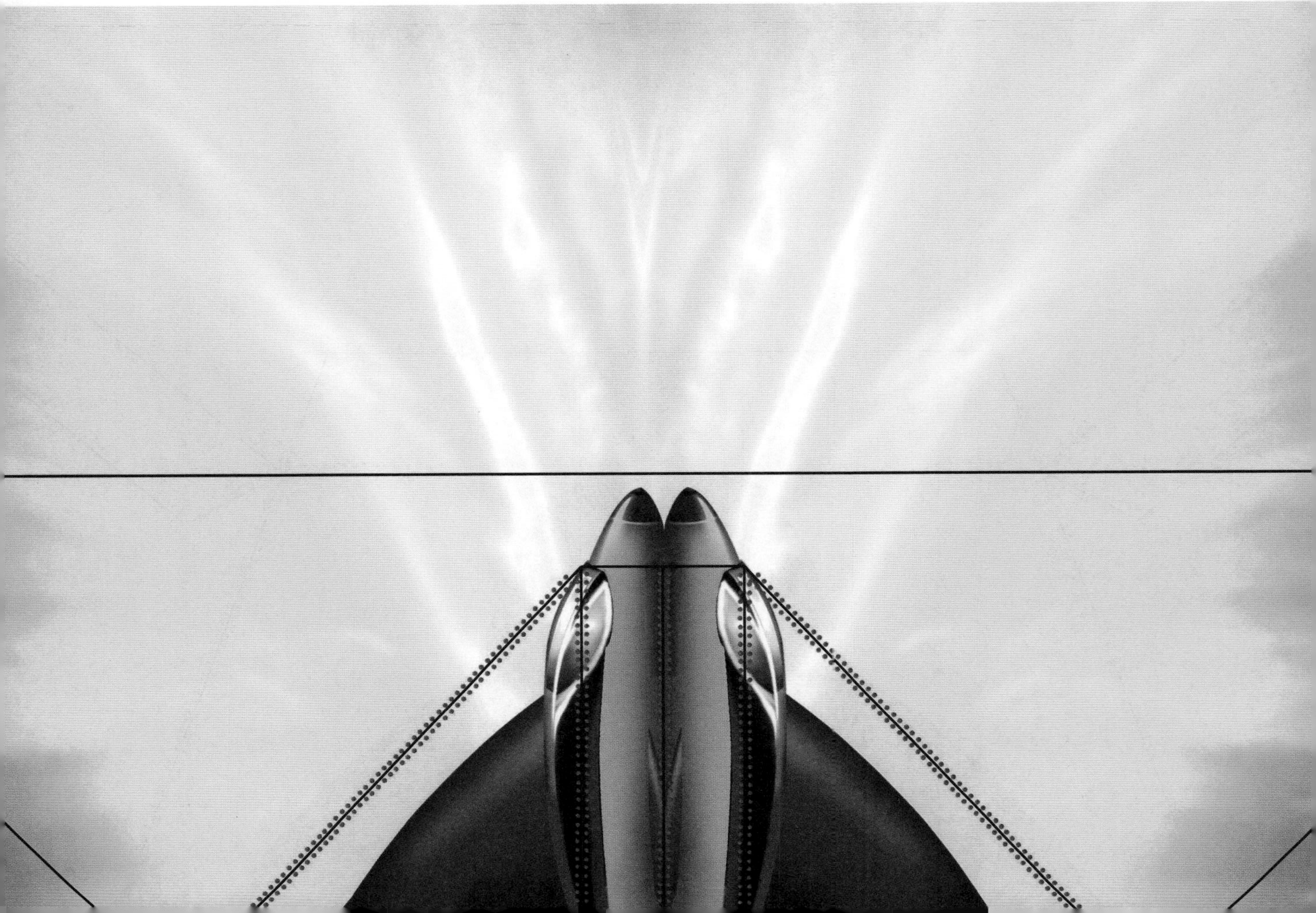

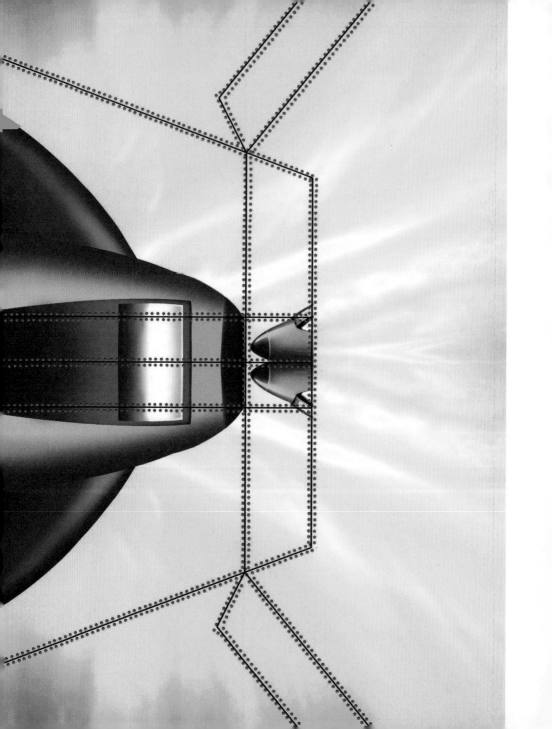

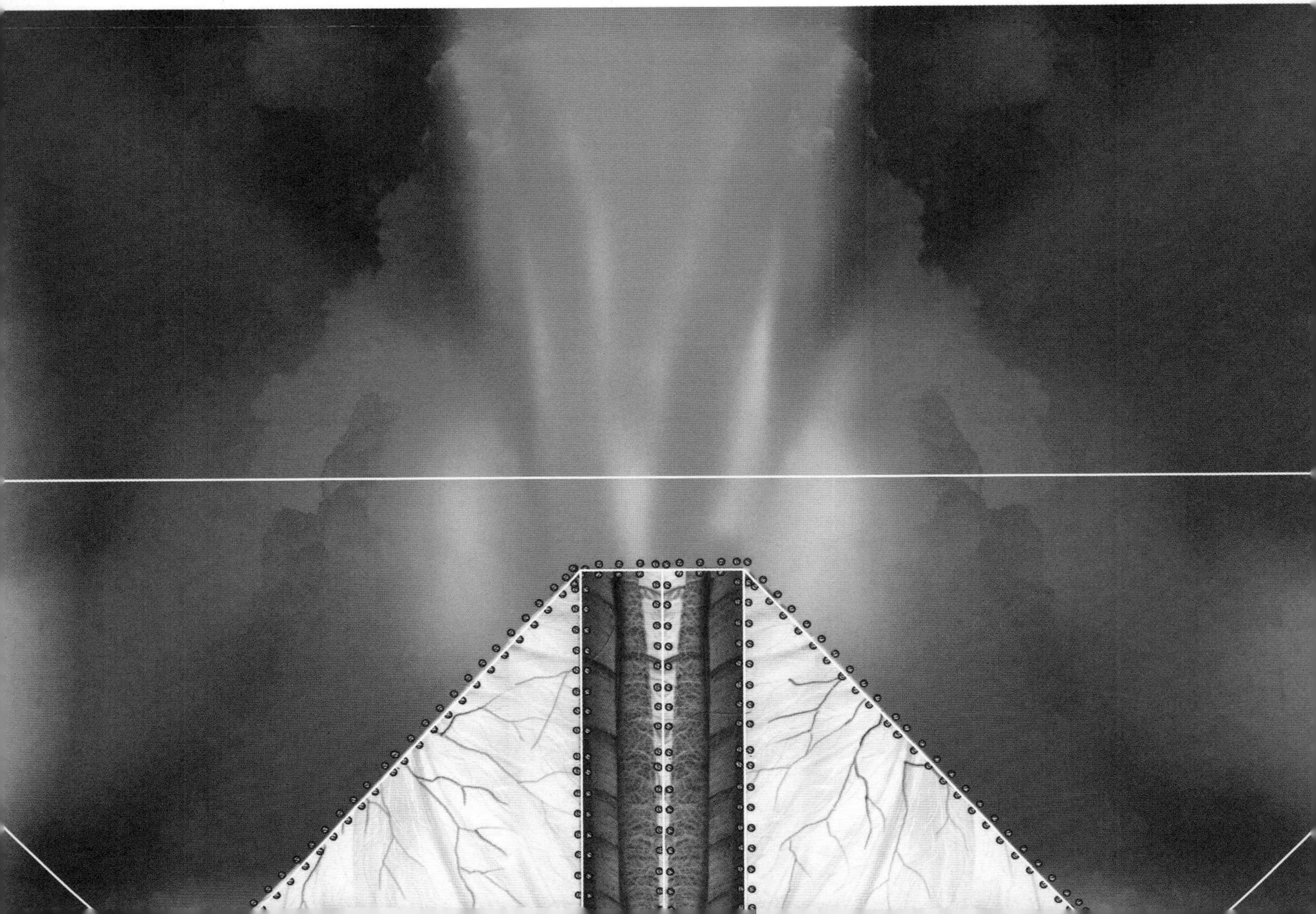

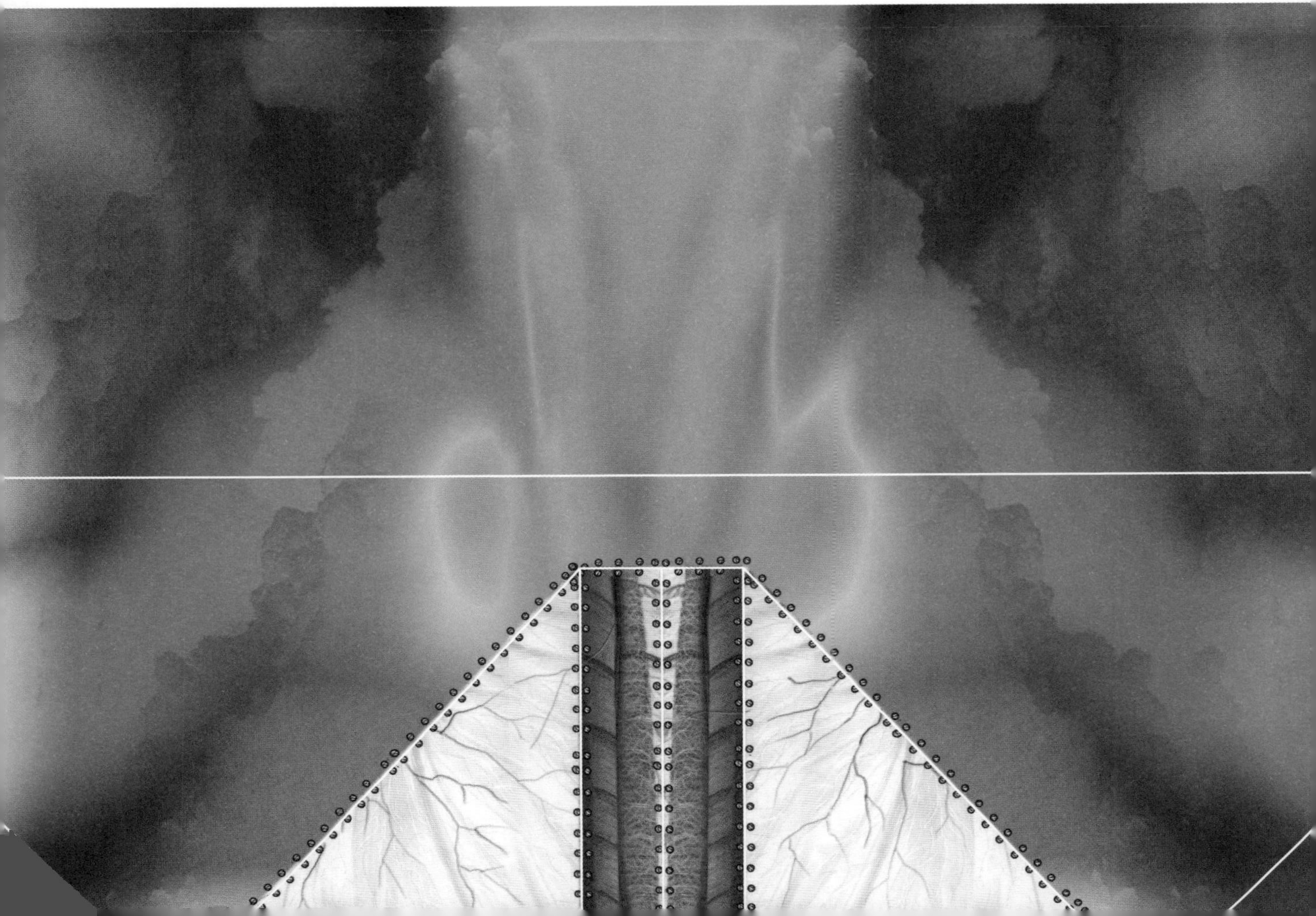

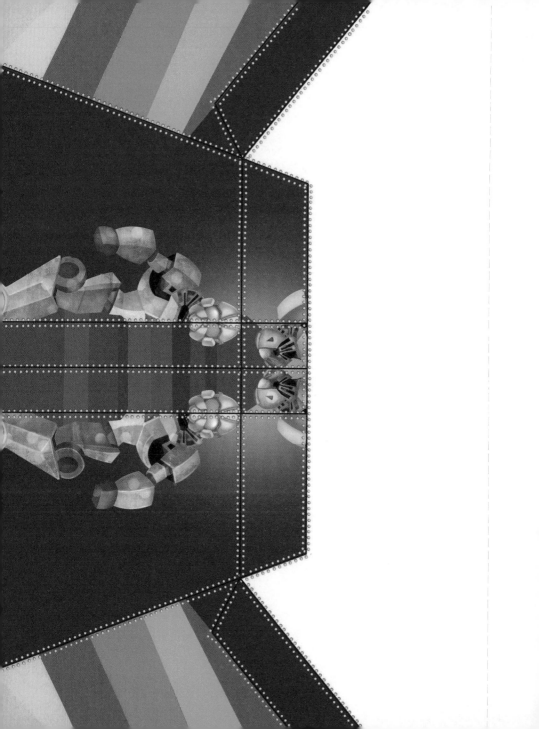

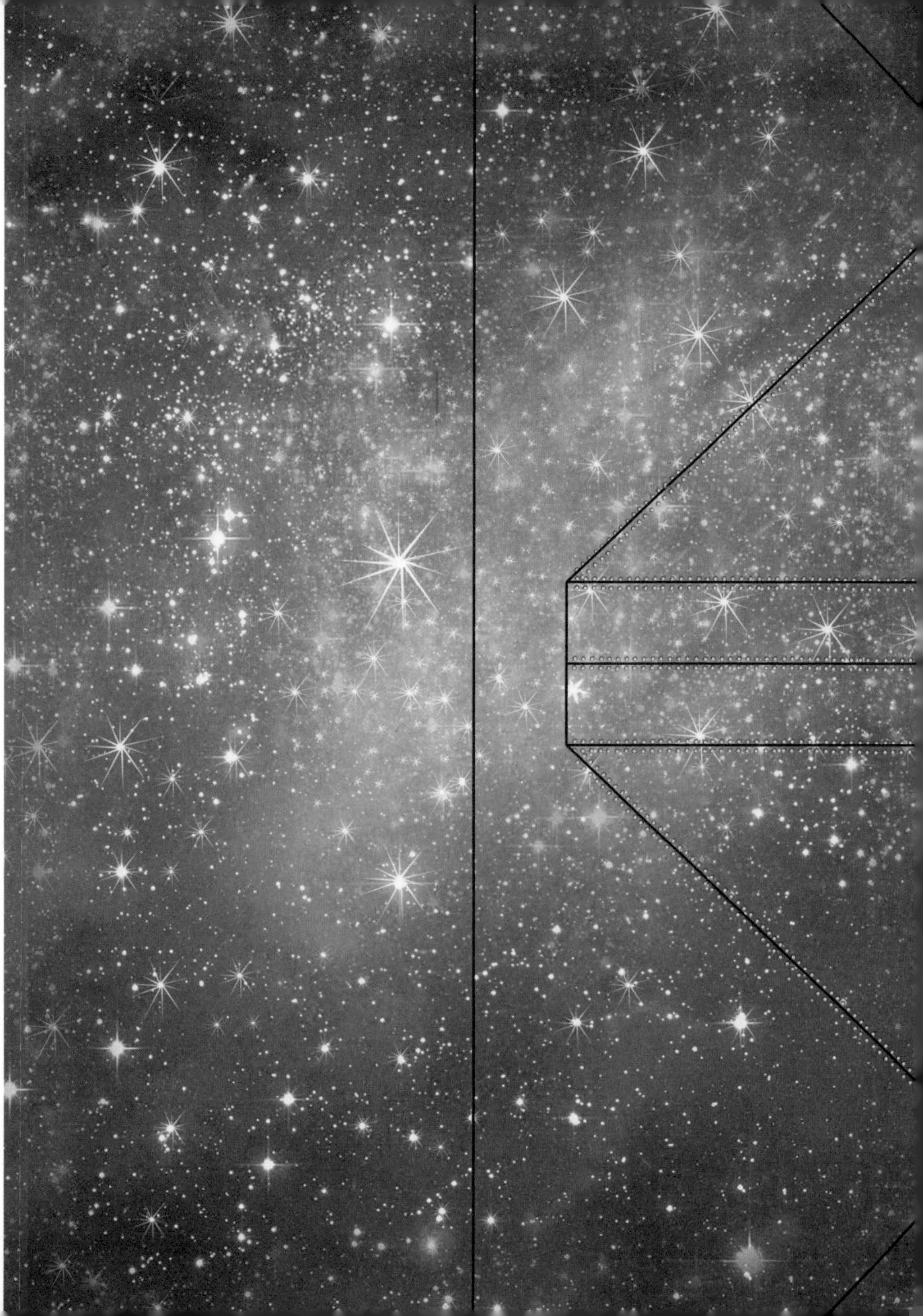

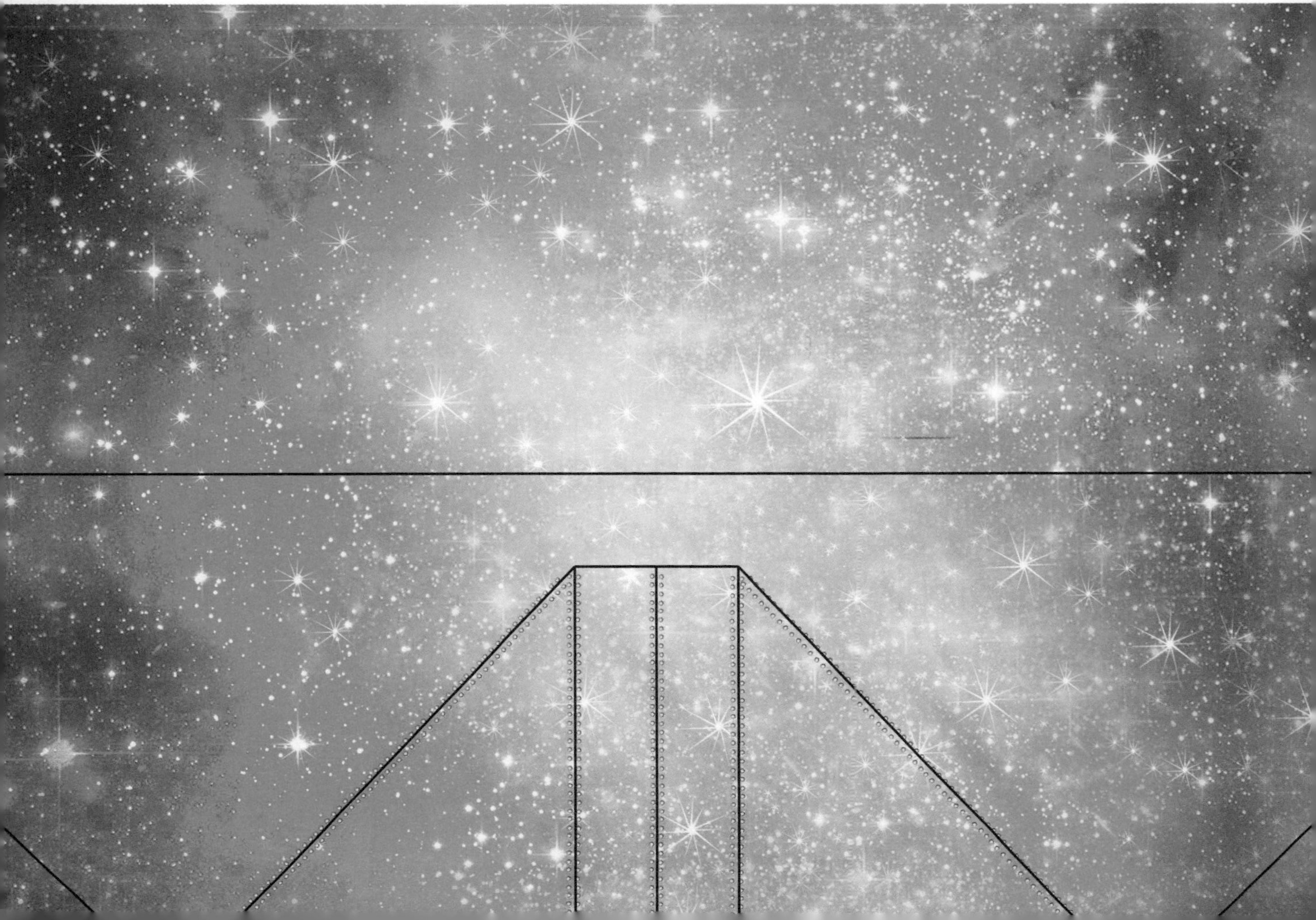

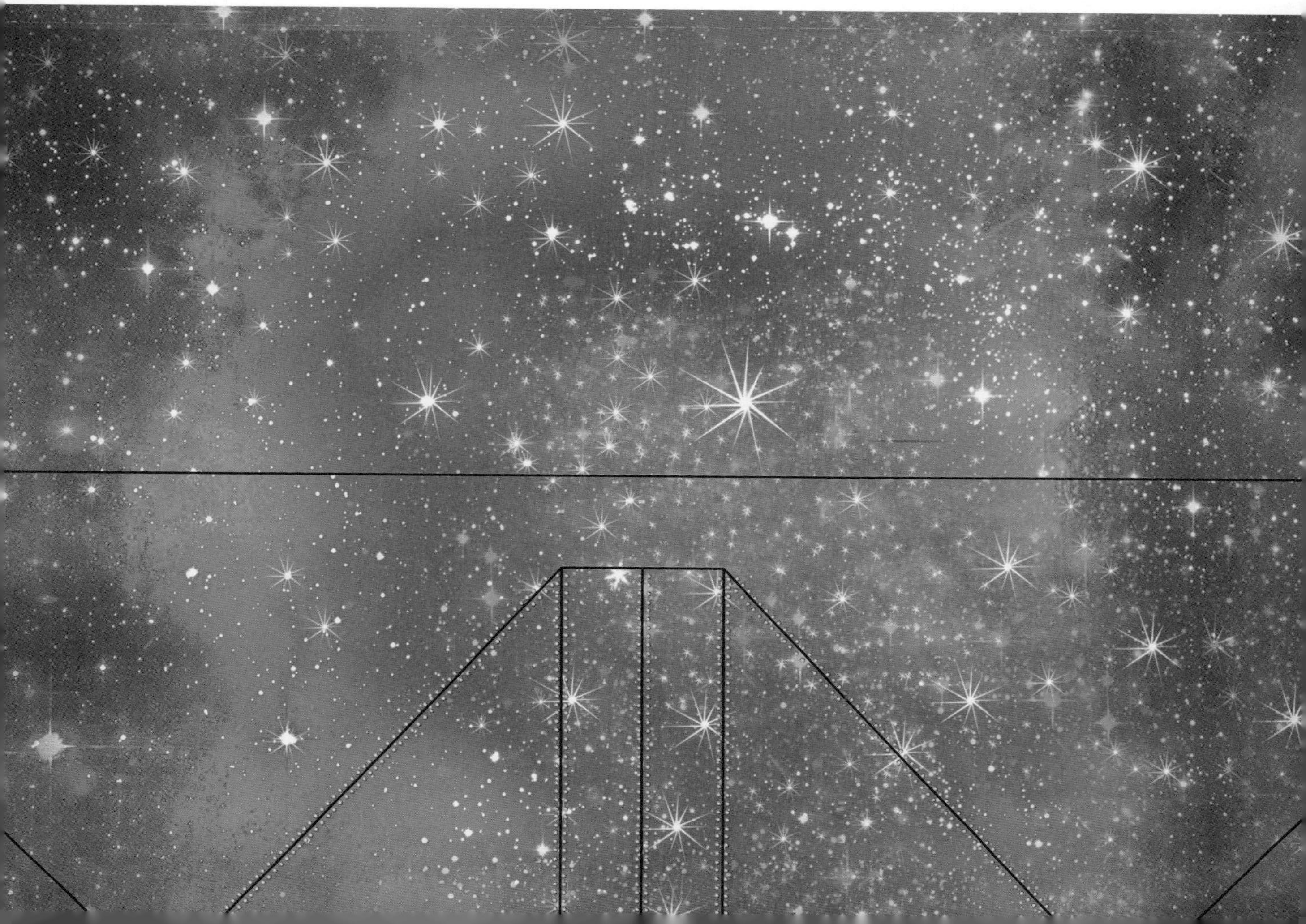

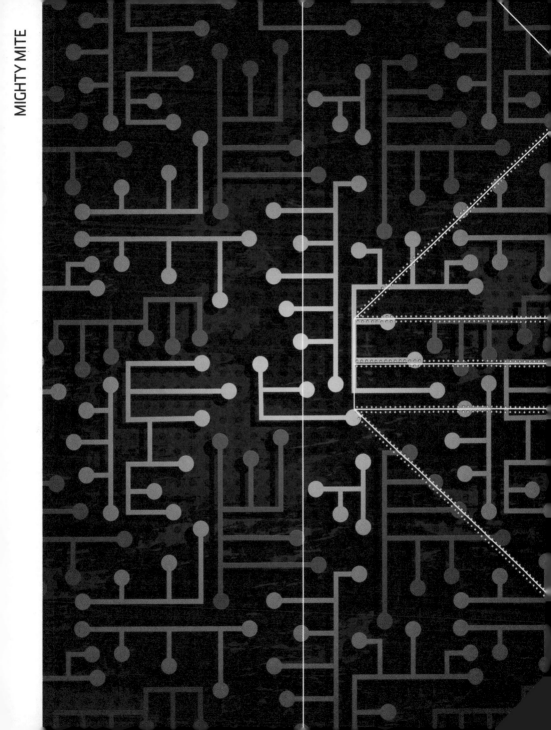

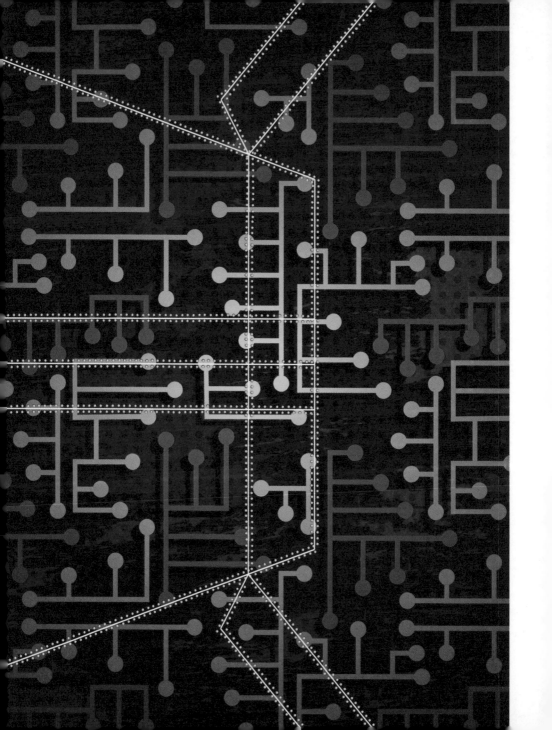

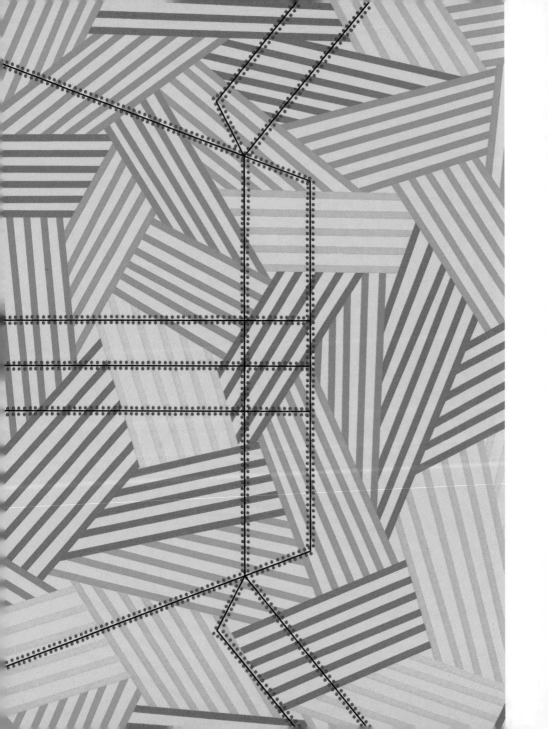

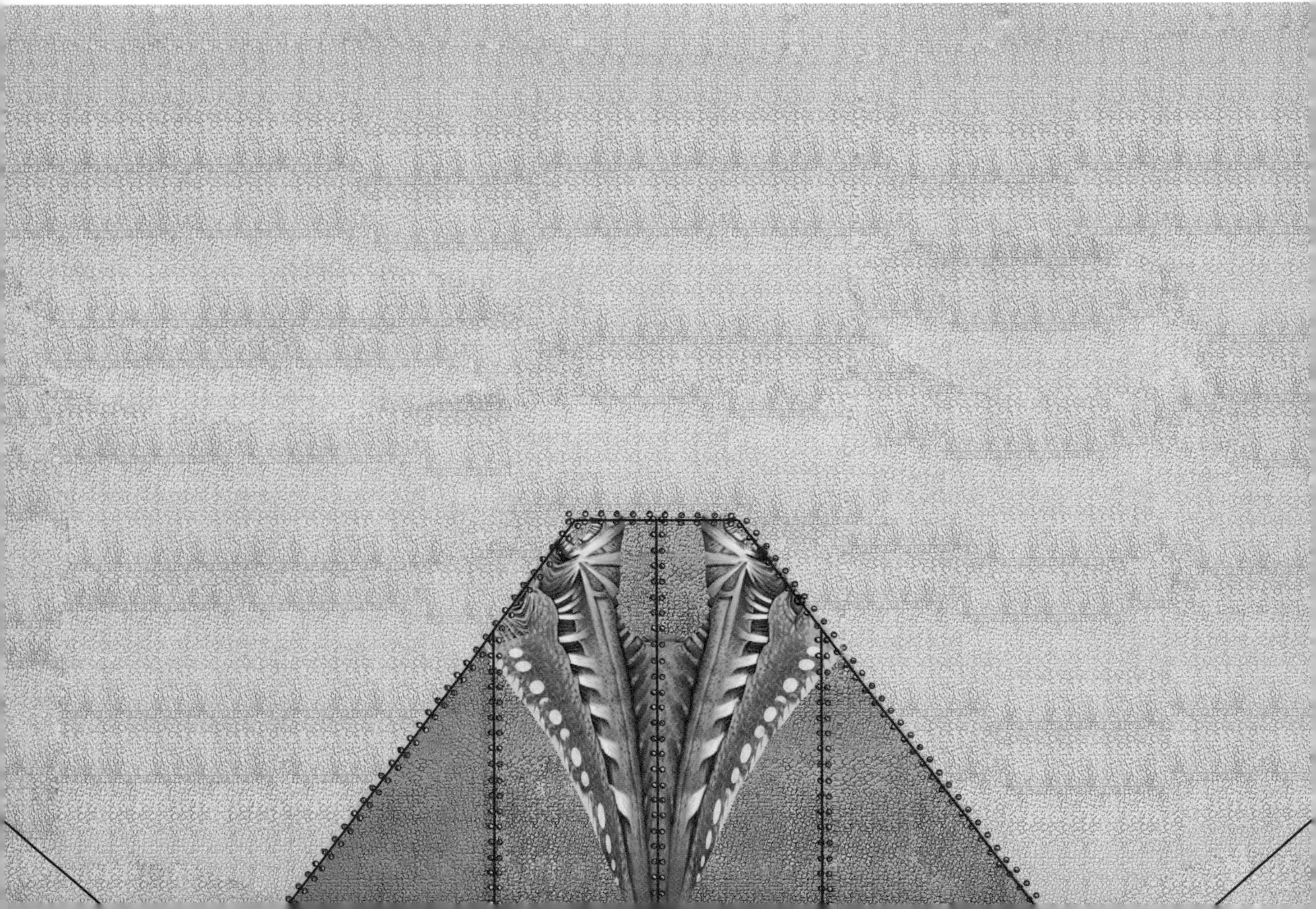

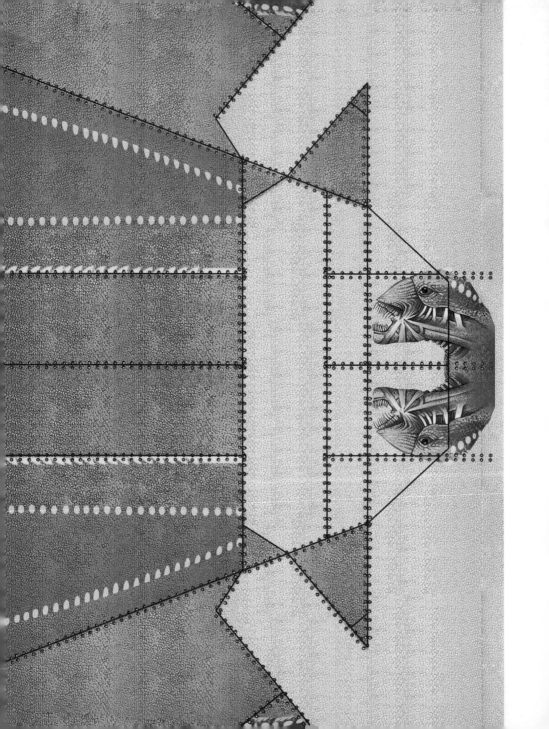

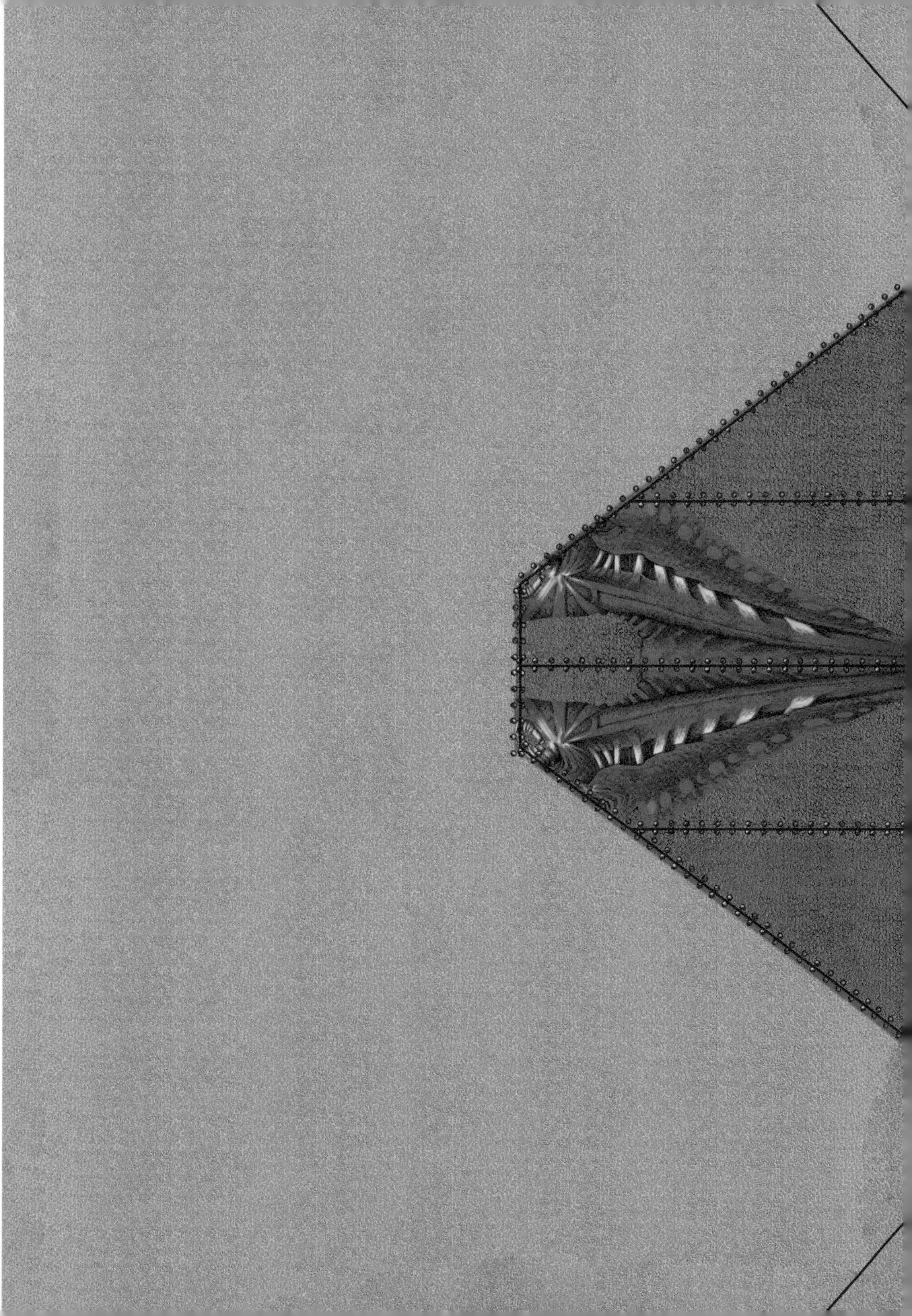

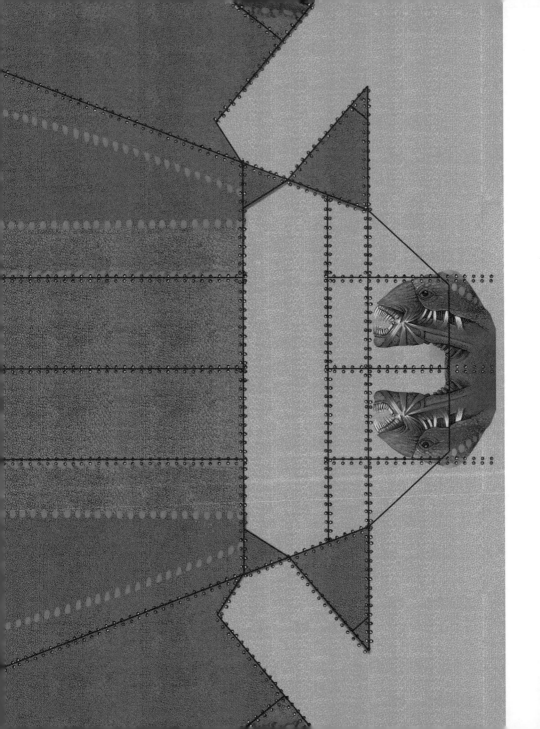

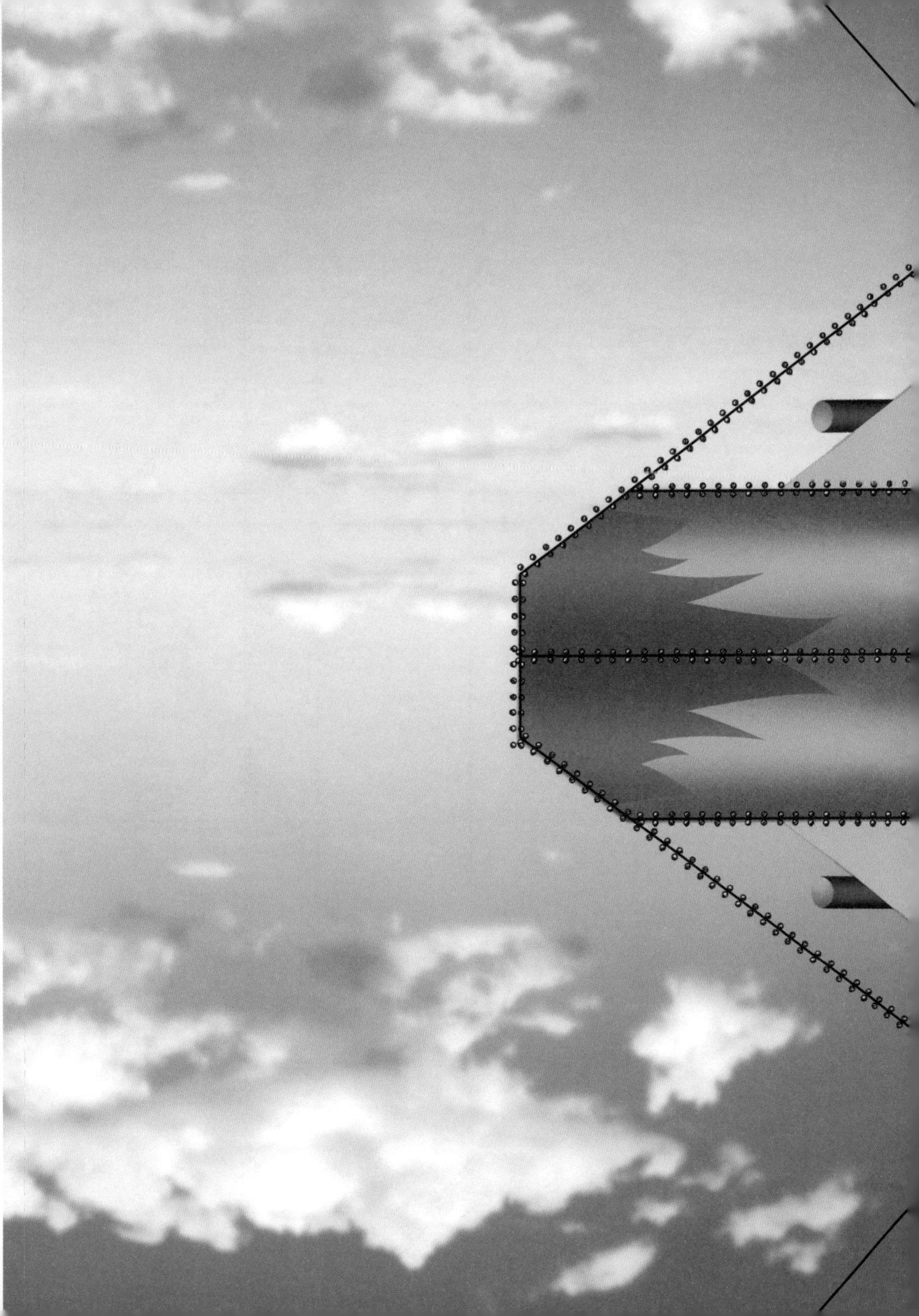

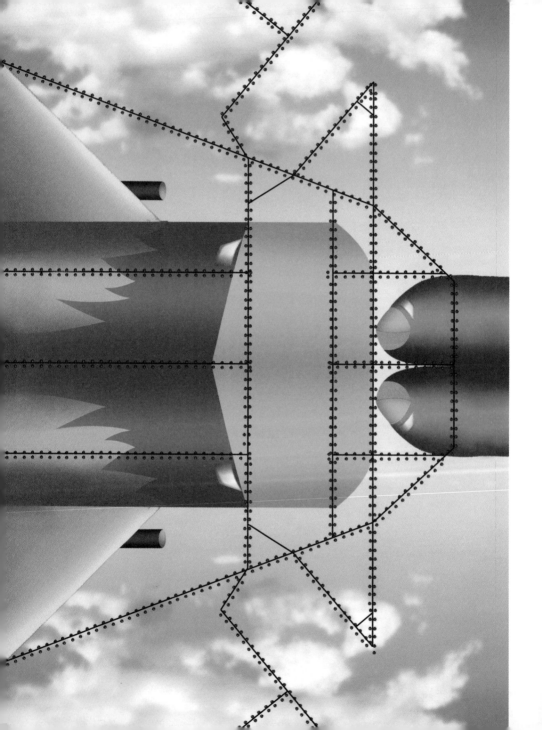

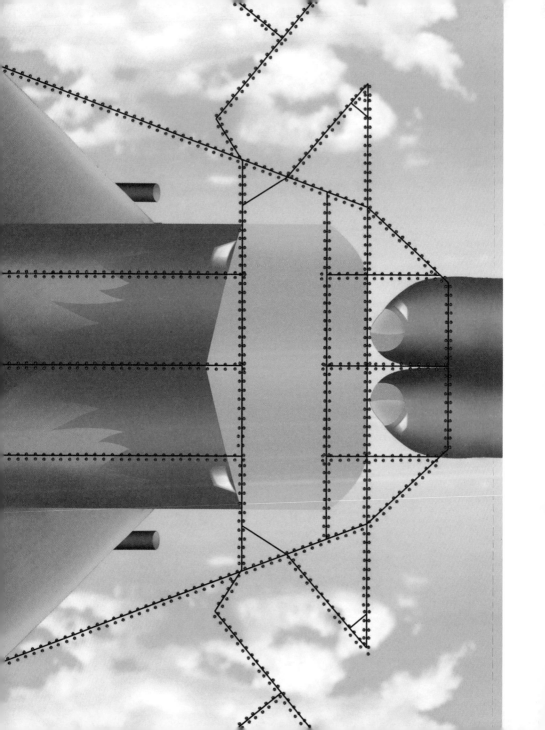

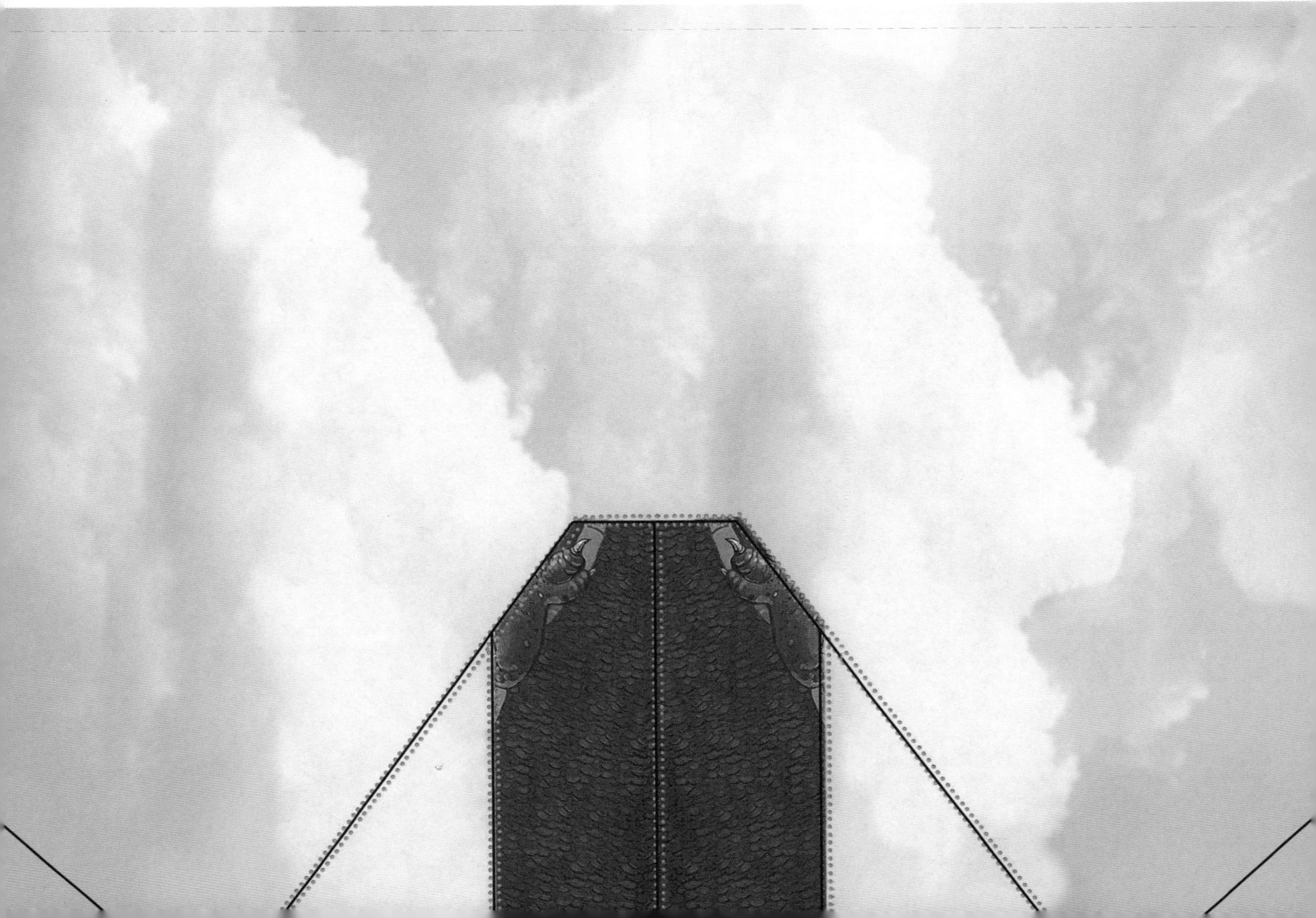

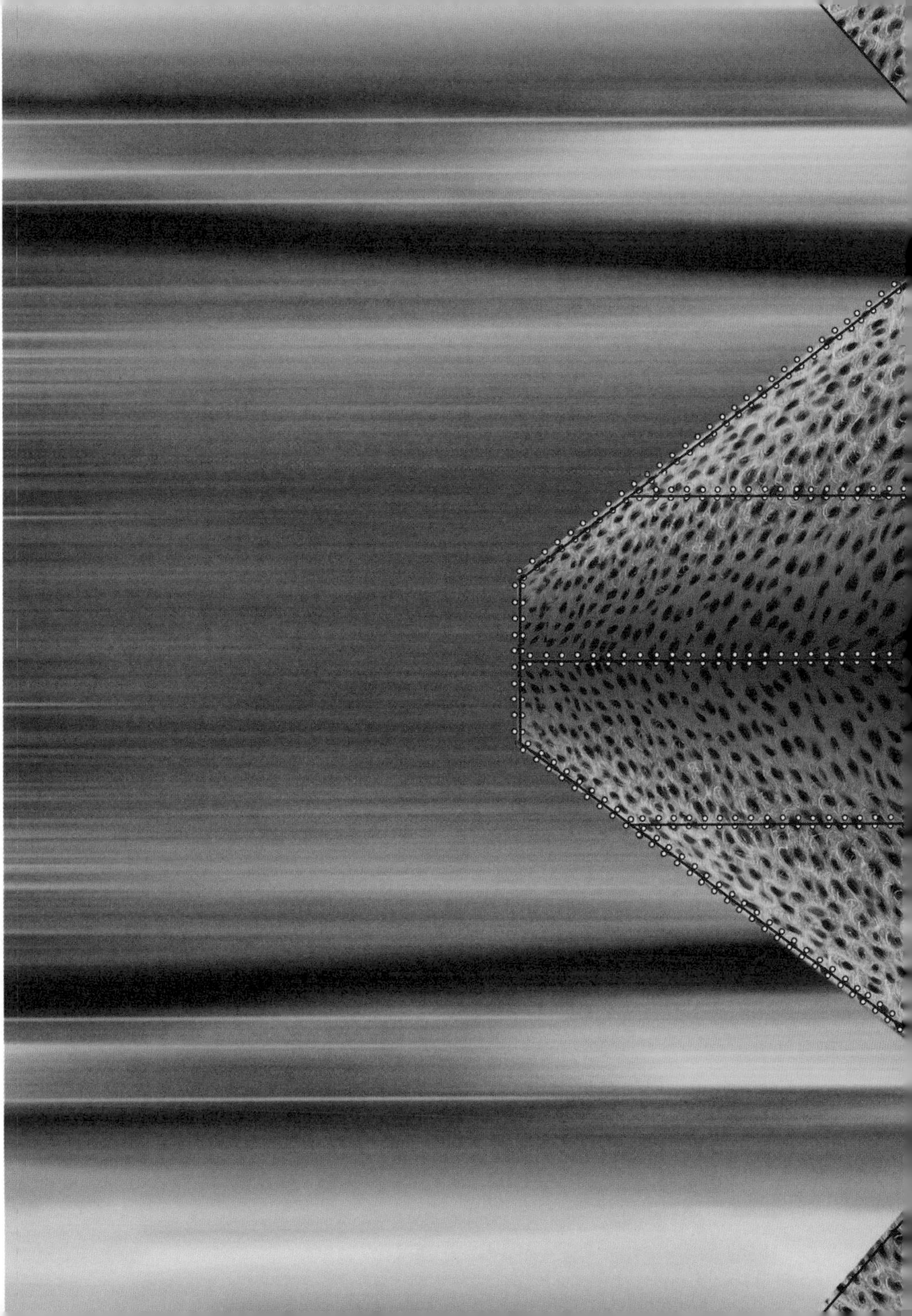

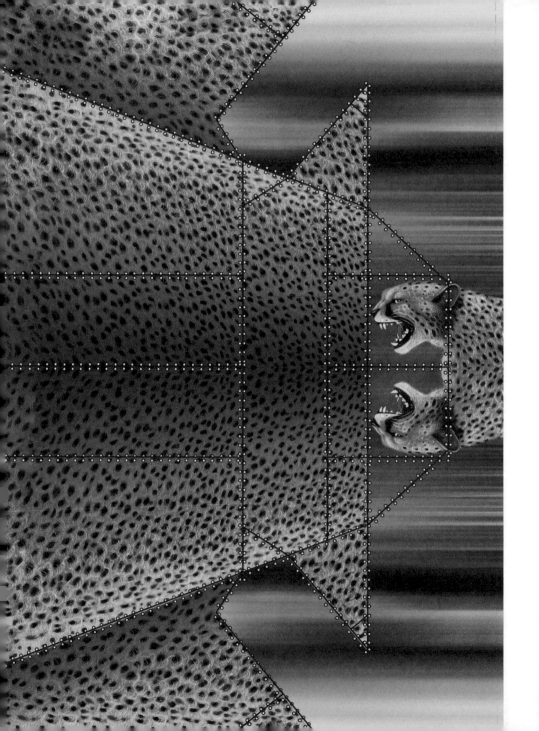

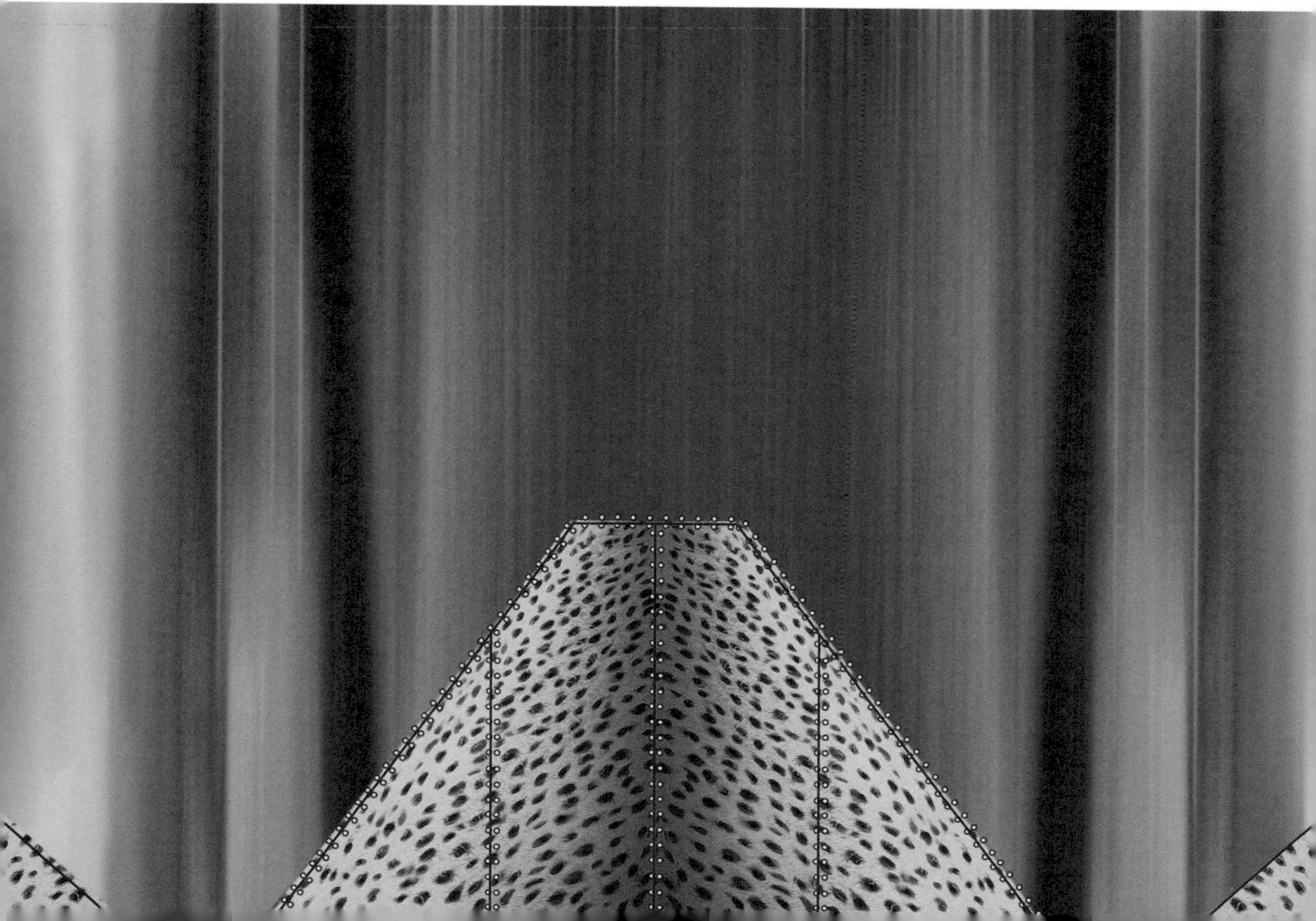

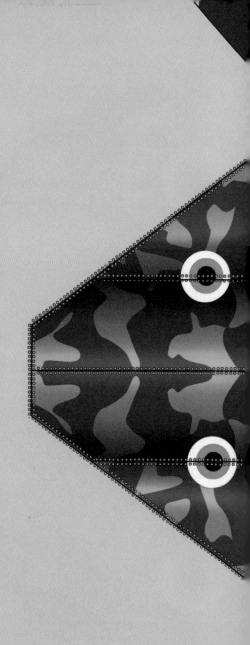

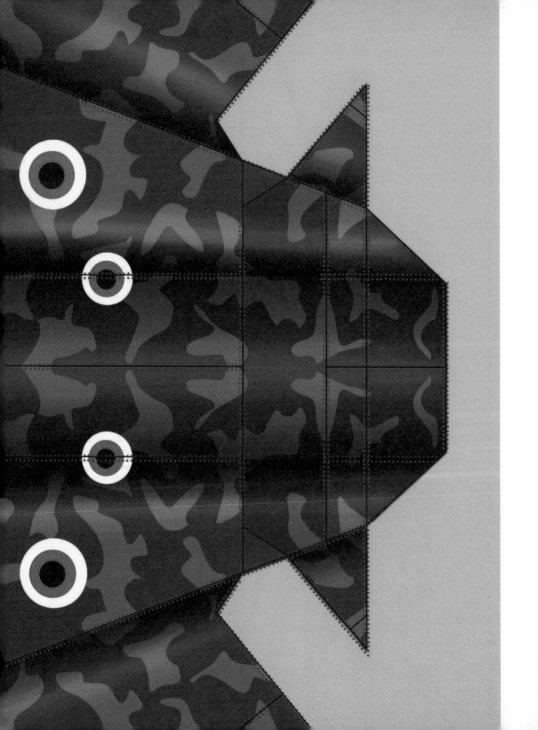

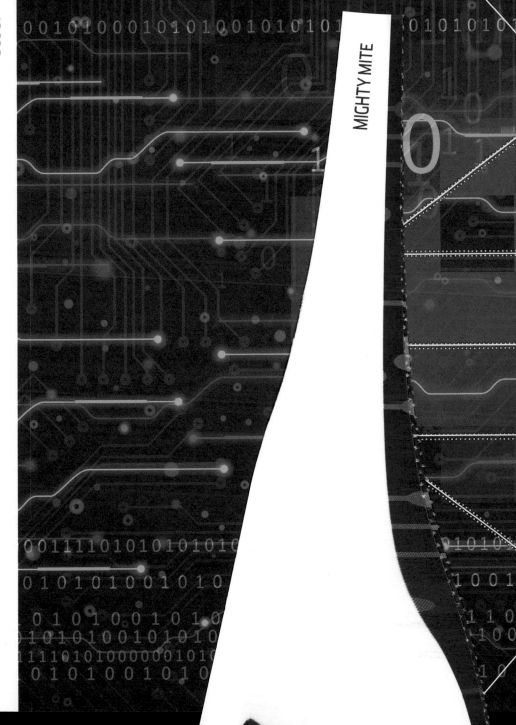

00101000101010010101010101010101

00111101010101010

0101010010101 0

0101001010

01010100101010

11110101000000101010

01010010101

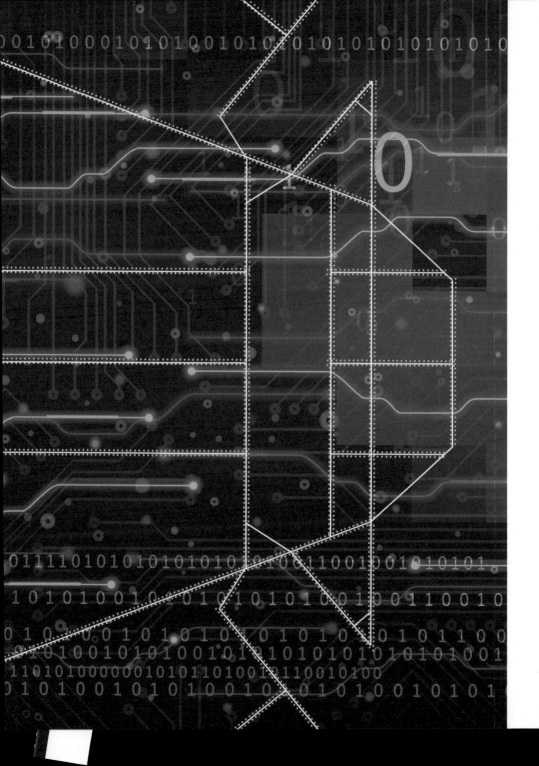

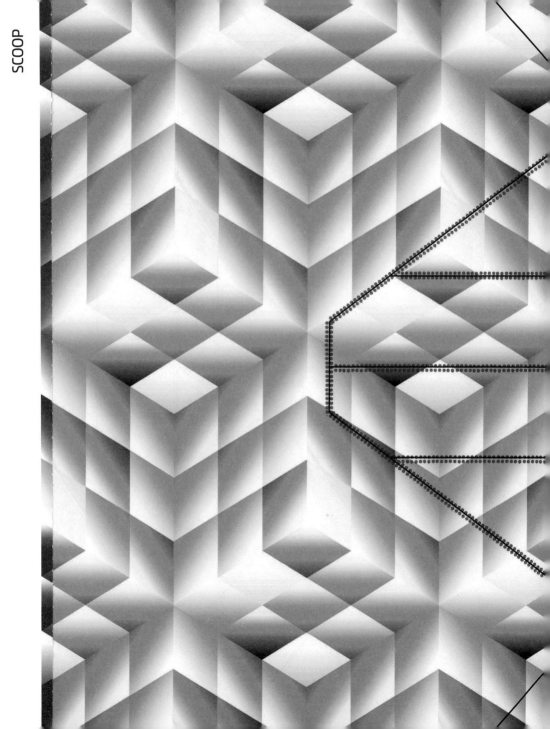

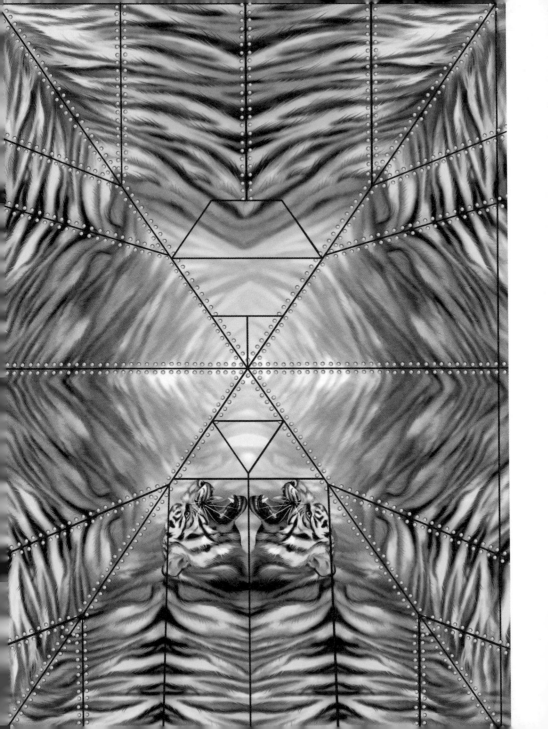

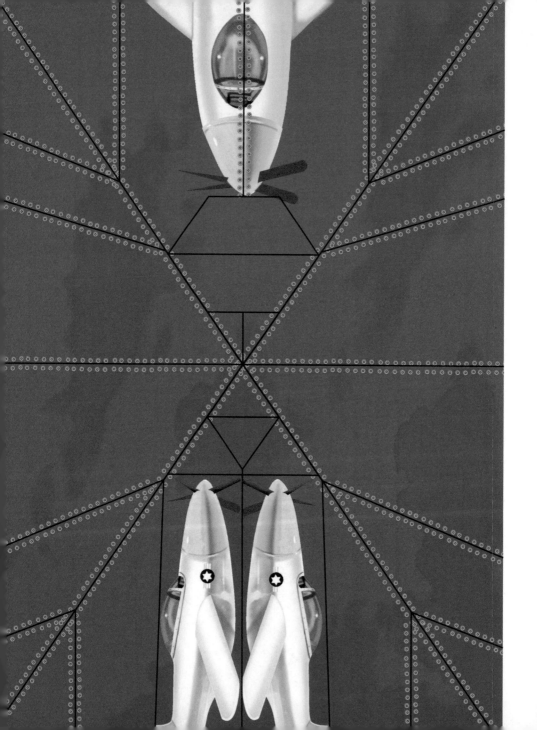

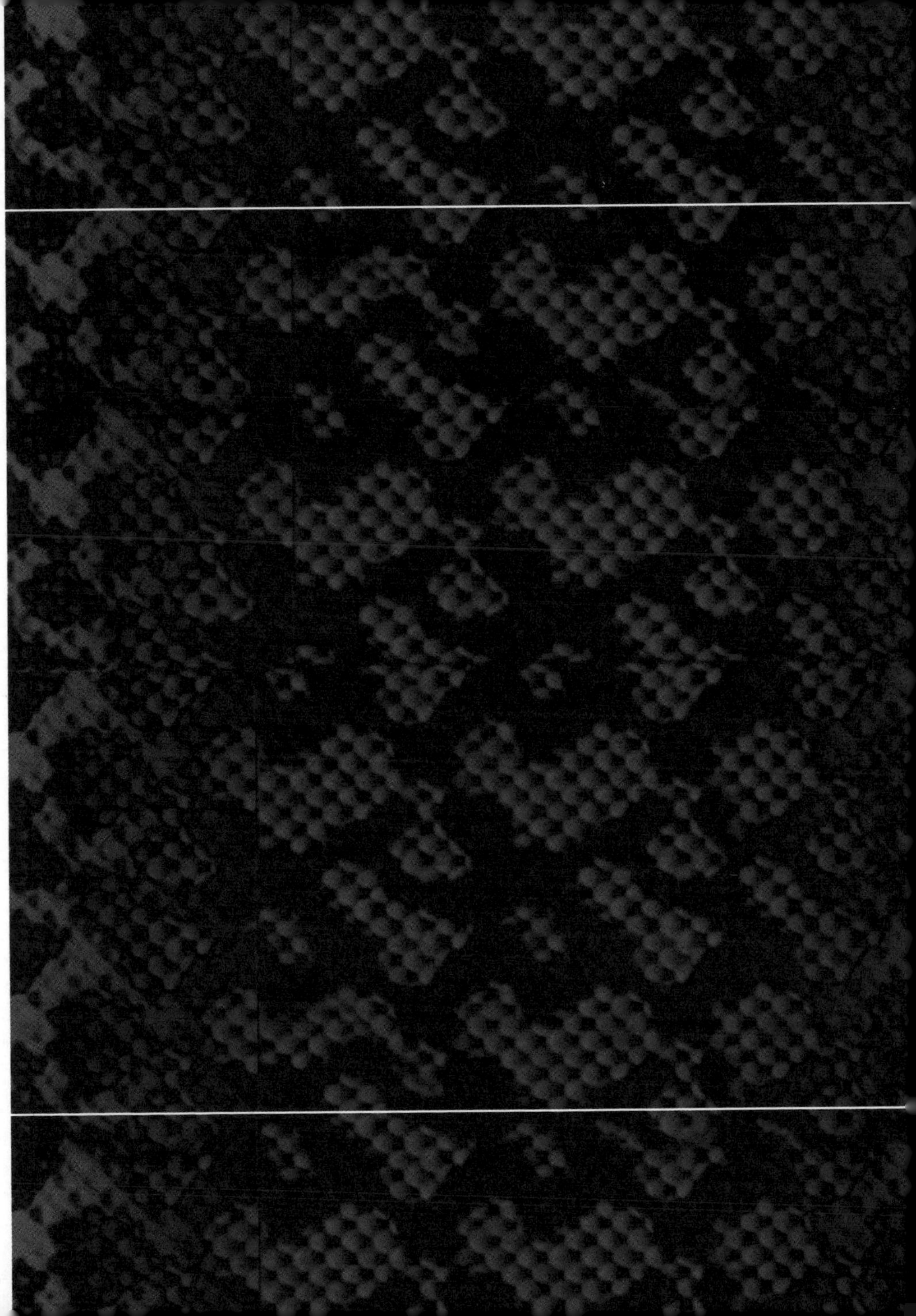

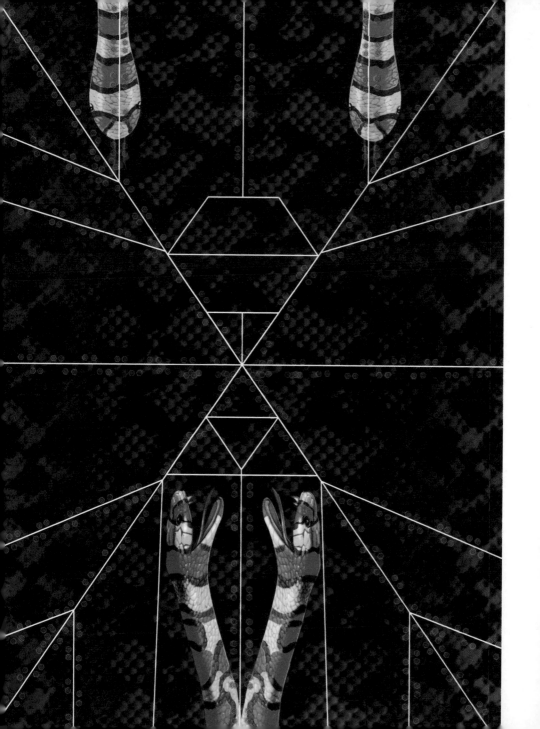

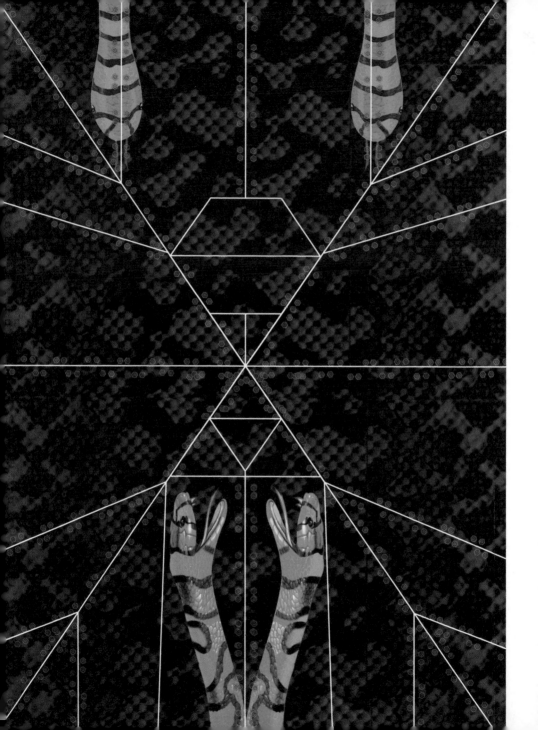

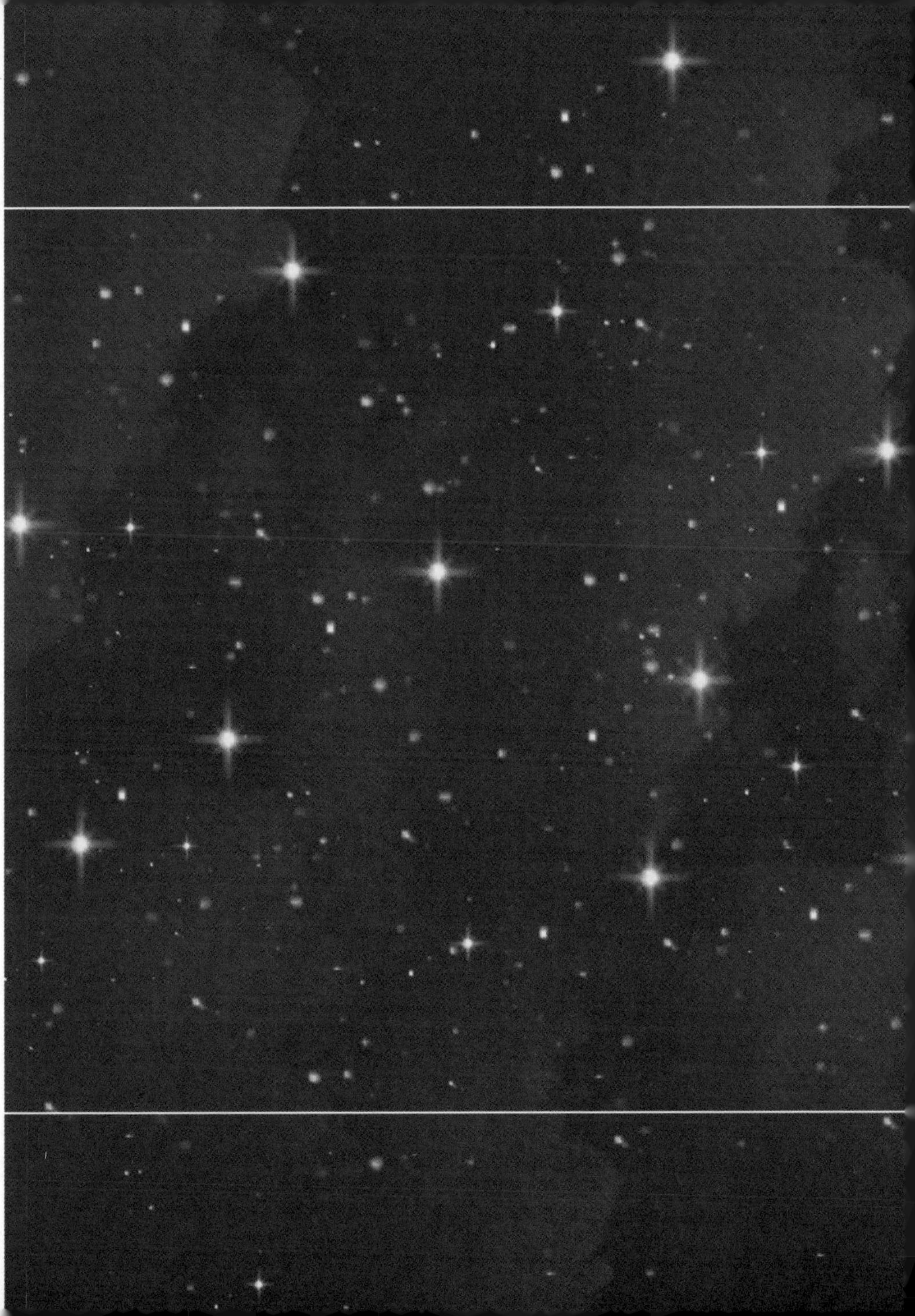

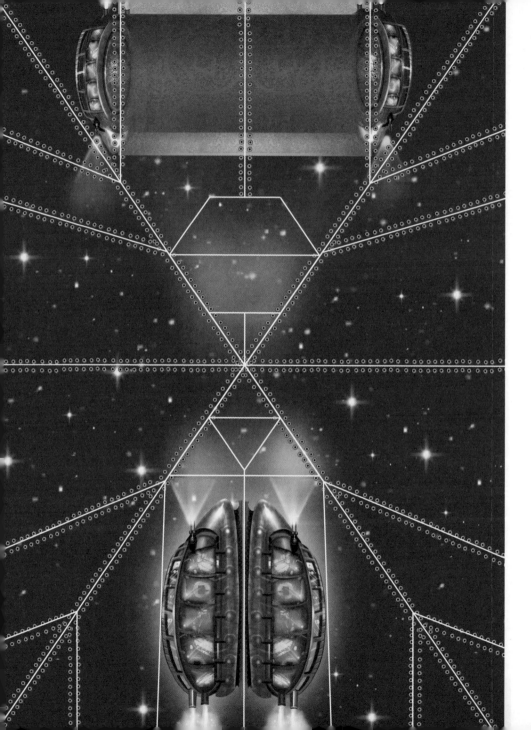

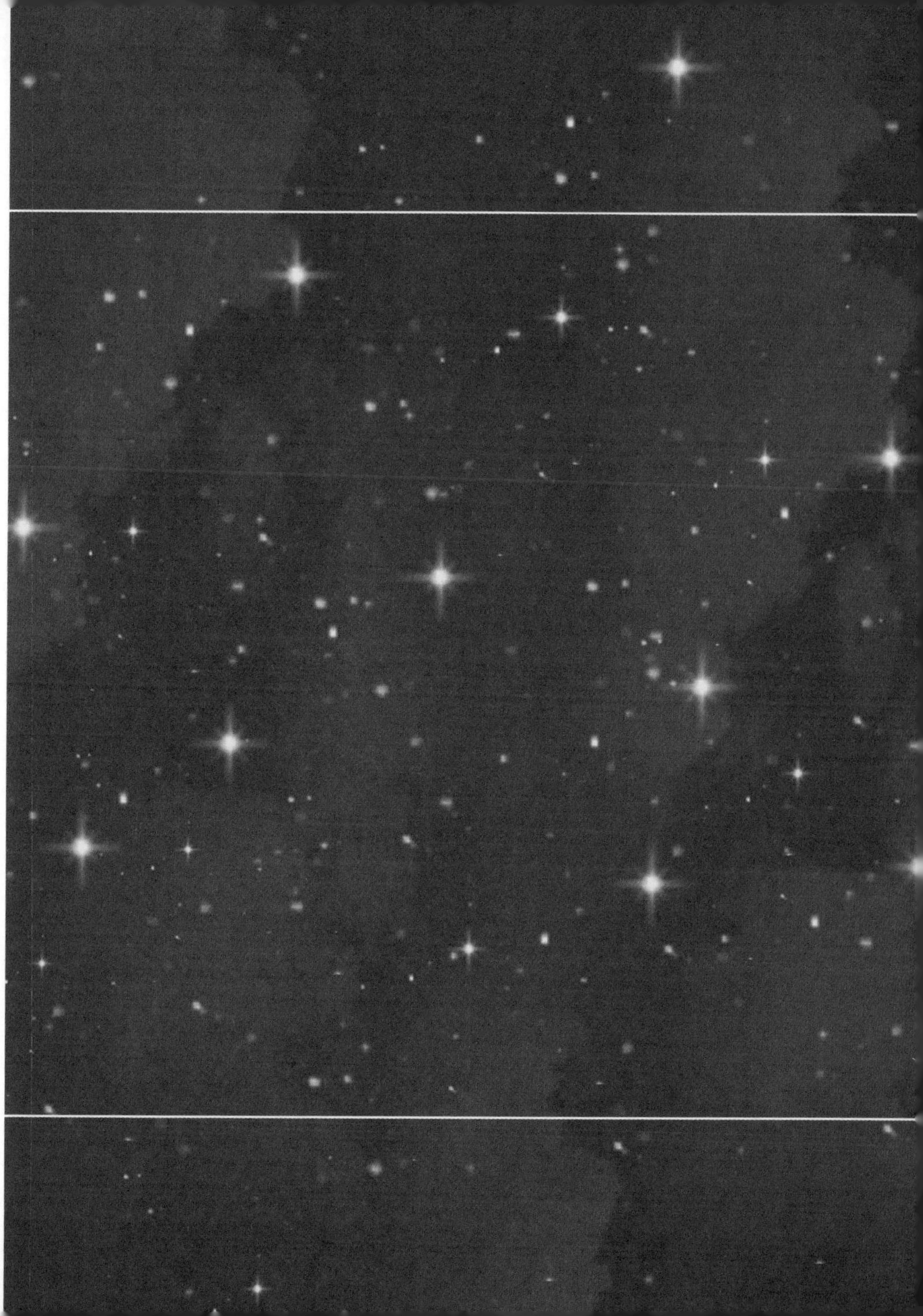

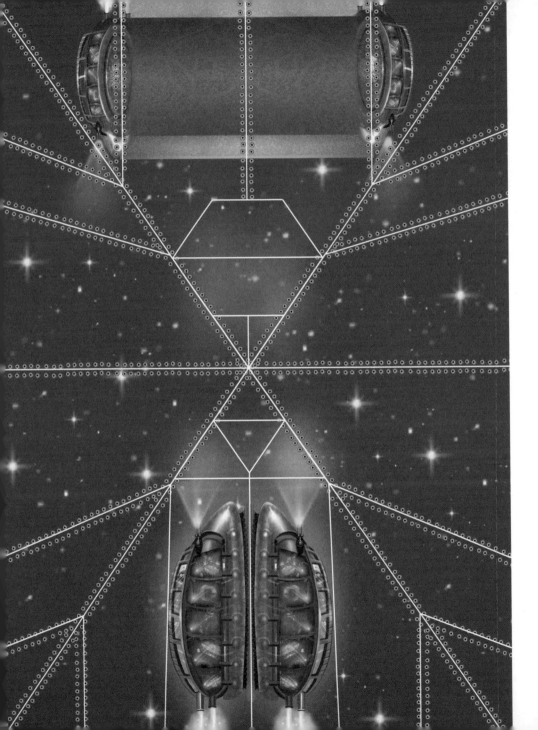

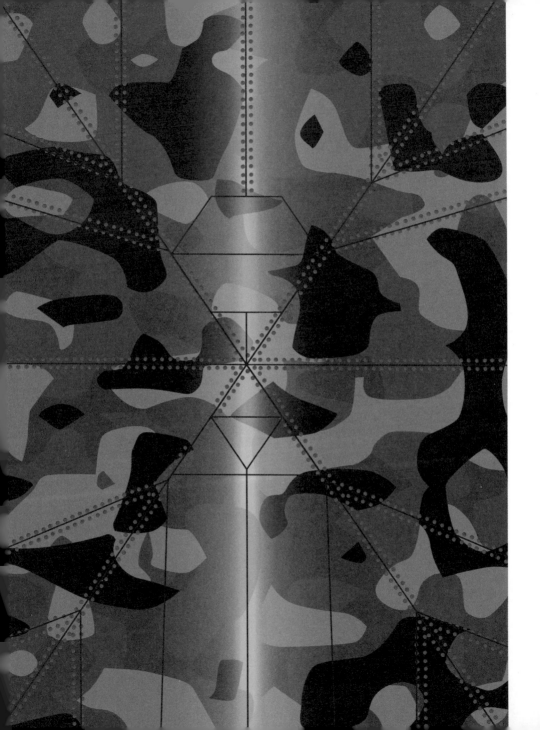

ALIEN LANDER

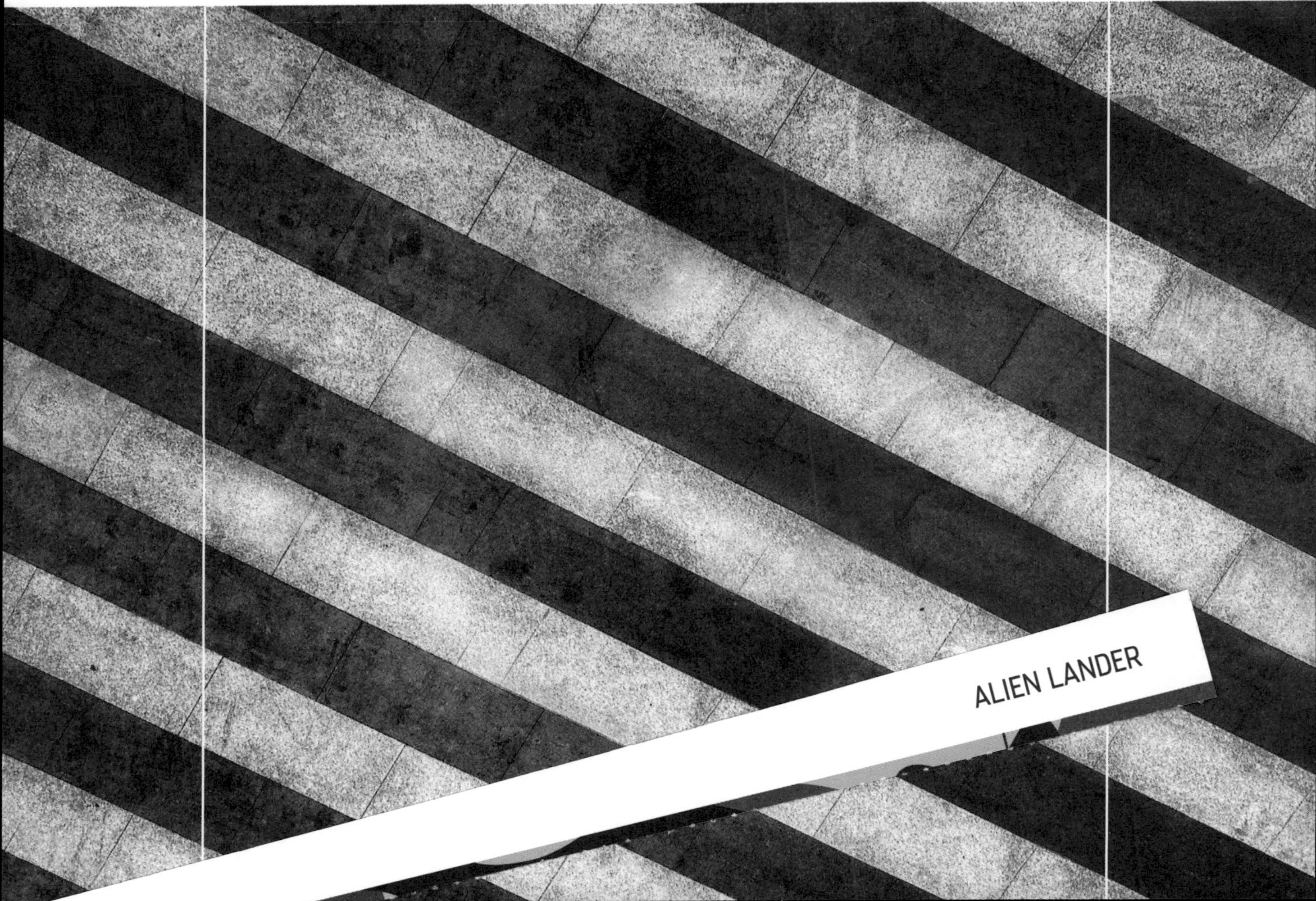

ALIEN LANDER

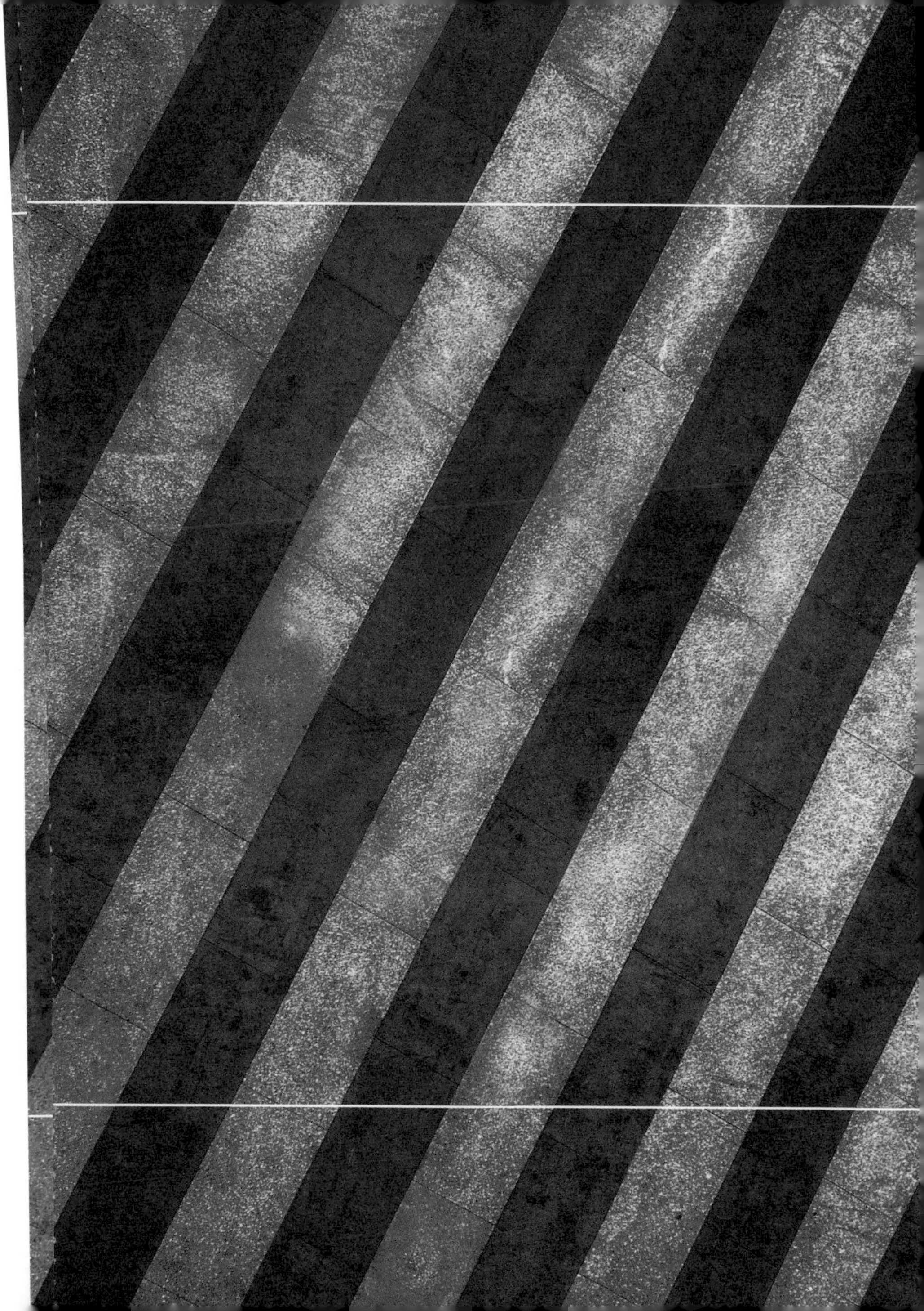

ALIEN LANDER

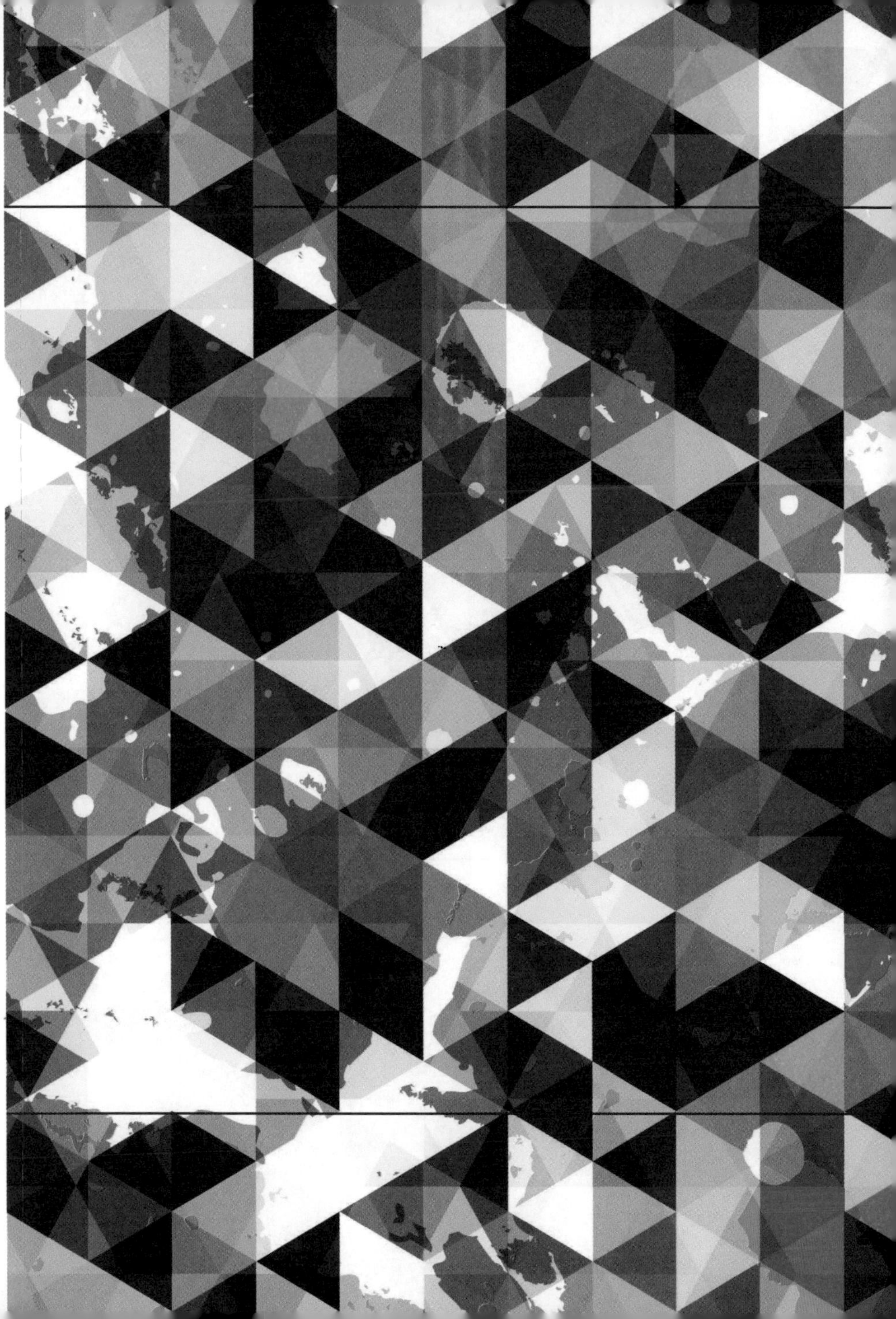

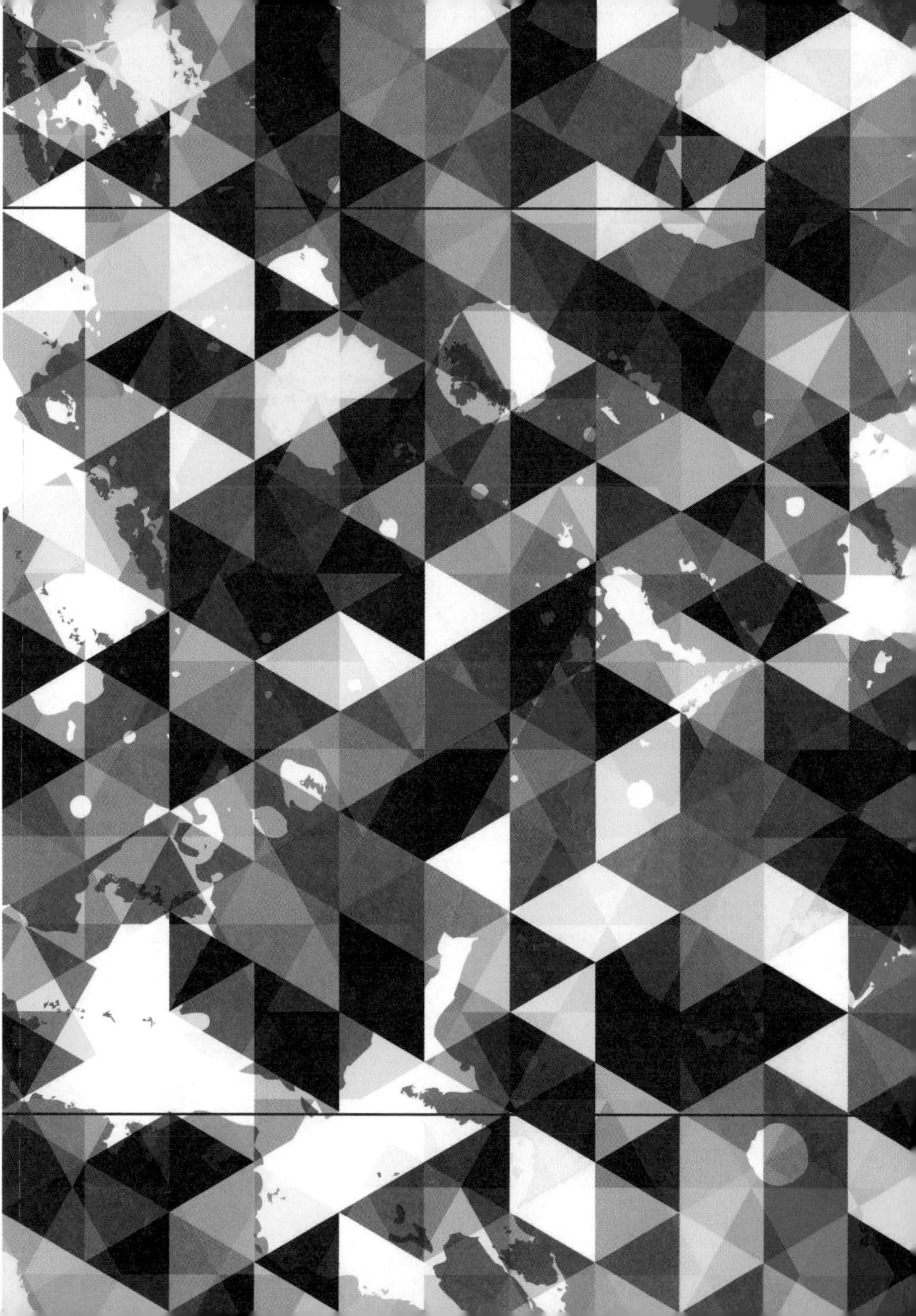

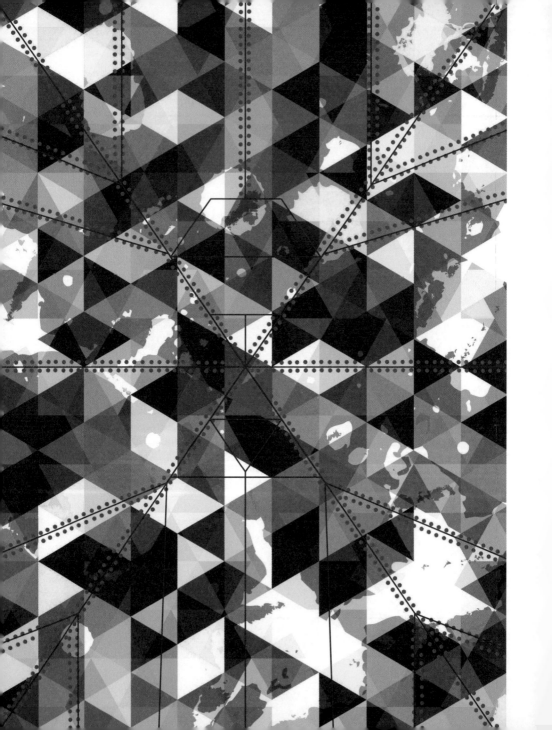

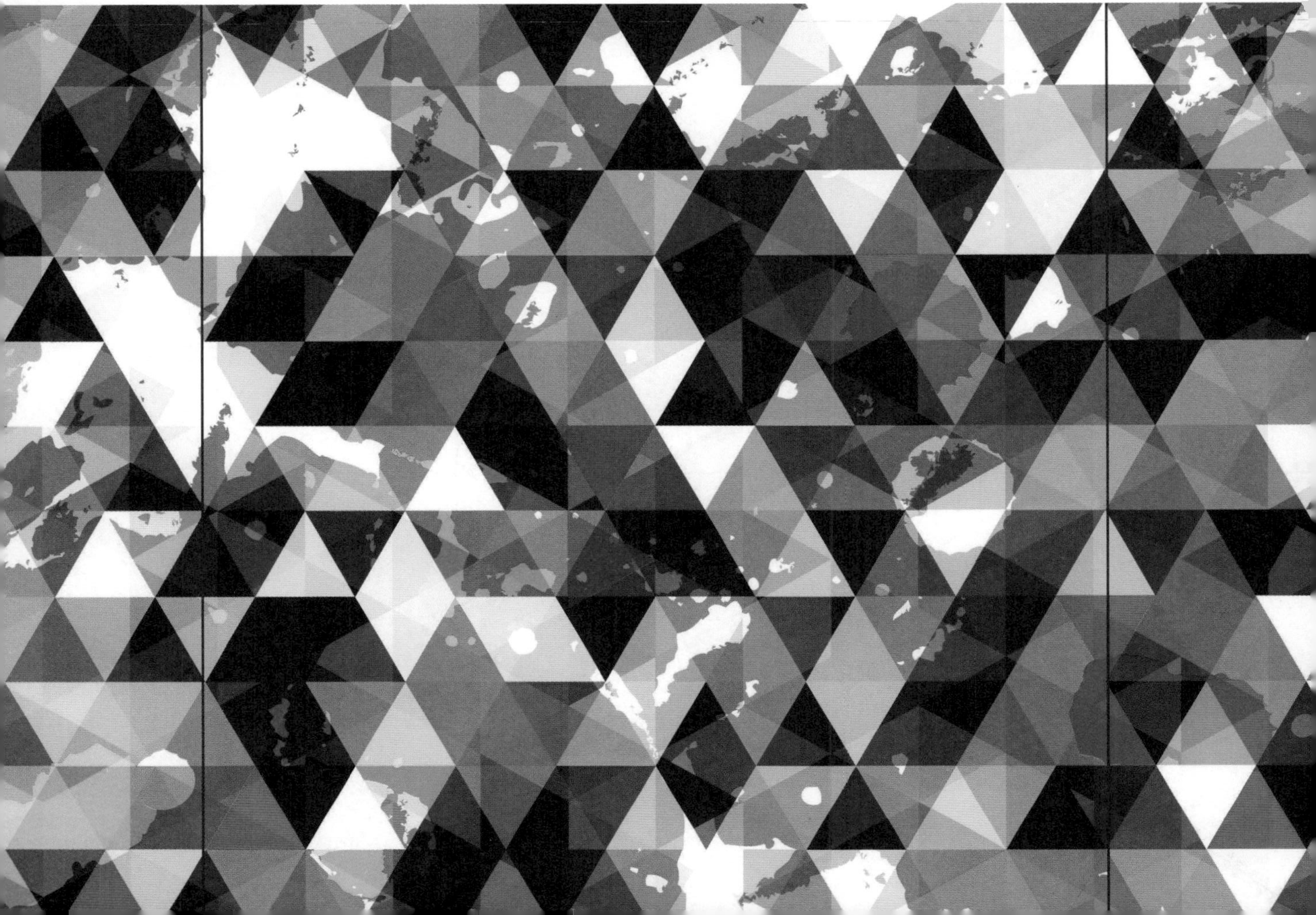

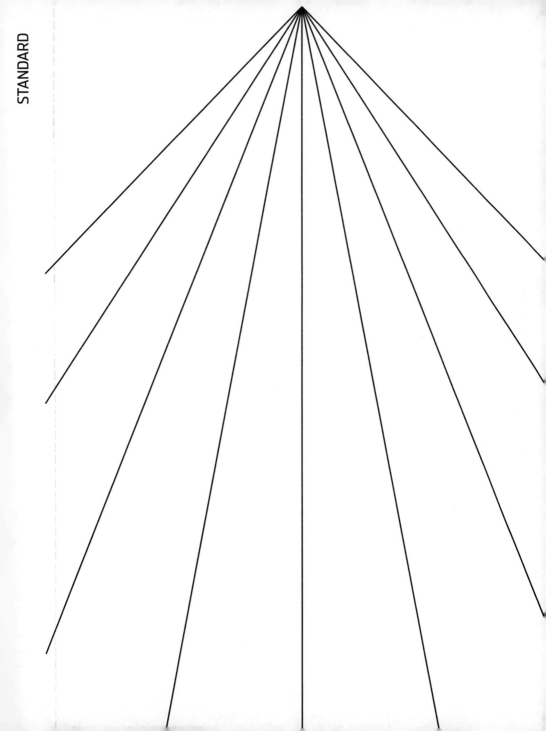

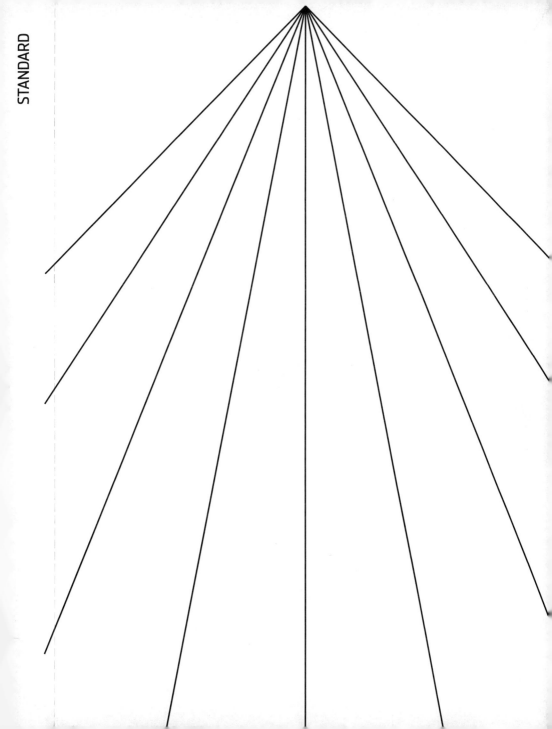

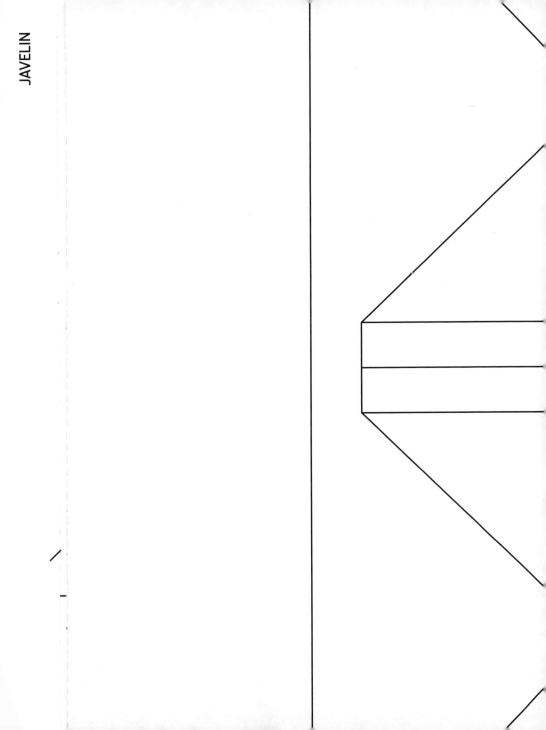

JAVELIN

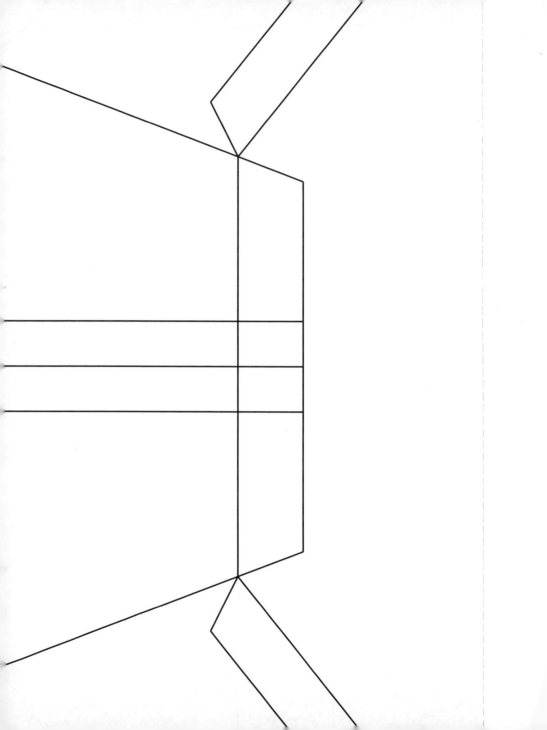

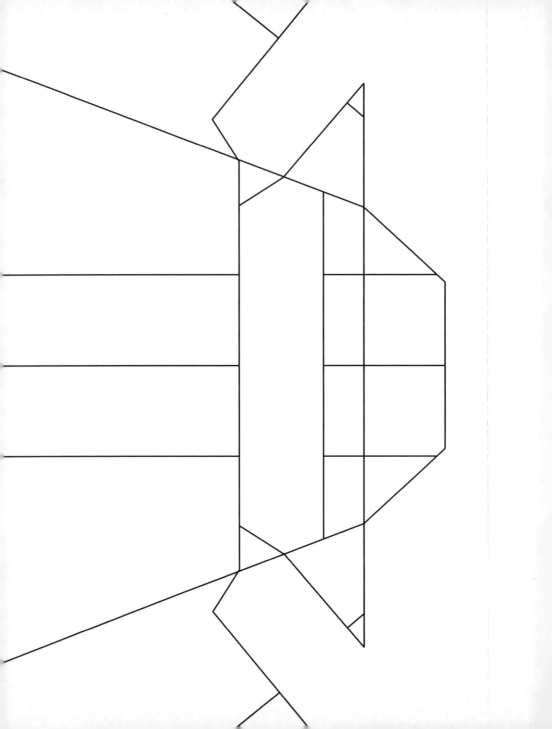

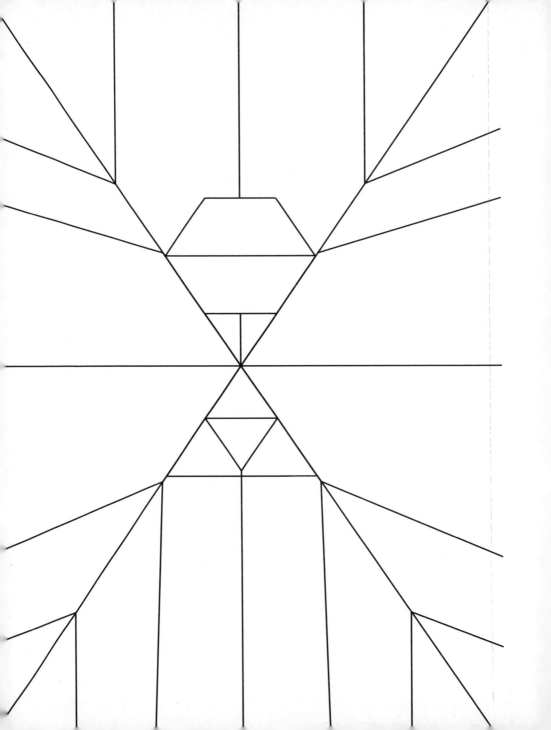